Travelers and Pleasure Seekers

WILL FIND AT OUR BOOK STORE,

372 Larimer Street, Denver,

NEW and ACCURATE MAPS of the TERRITORY, showing all the principal places and routes of travel.

SEVEN HUNDRED DIFFERENT STEREOSCOPIC VIEWS of cities, towns, parks, mines and mountains, by the best artists.

A GREAT VARIETY OF CHOICE BOOKS, full of descriptions of scenery, details and statistics of Colorado, its growth, attractions of climate, and resources.

THE WORKS of ALL THE POPULAR AUTHORS, in paper covers, for travelers' use.

TERRITORIAL AND STATES PAPERS AND MAGAZINES.

A Complete Assortment of DIARIES, POCKET MEMO-RANDA BOOKS, and All Kinds of Stationery.

RICHARDS & CO.

Summering

in

Colorado.

Charles Harrington

DENVER:
RICHARDS & CO., PUBLISHERS,
No. 372 LARIMER STREET.
1874.

Entered according to Act of Congress, in the year 1874, by

RICHARDS & CO.,

In the office of the Librarian of Congress at Washington.

DENVER: PRESS OF WM. N. BYERS

INTRODUCTION.

WE believe the tourist will find in this volume everything essential to convey a comprehensive idea of the routes of summer travel in Colorado, the scenery that meets the eye at every point of note, the pleasure resorts, and the delightful experiences of mountaineering. It has been the desire of the writer to group these matters together in a manner that should be at once instructive and entertaining.

THE PUBLISHERS.

DENVER, May 1874.

CONTENTS.

I.	A Fortnight in Denver	9
II.	Into the American Switzerland	19
III.	A Week in the Gold Region	29
IV.	To Estes' Park and Up Long's Peak	39
V.	Boulder Canon	49
VI.	Idaho Springs and the Hot Baths	57
VII.	To Georgetown and Vicinity	65
VIII.	Sauntering in Middle Park	77
IX.	South Park and Twin Lakes	87
X.	The Garden of the Gods	97
XI.	Manitou Springs and Pike's Peak	105
XII.	A Trip to Glen Eyrie	113
XIII.	To Cheyenne Canon	121
XIV.	Southern Colorado	127
XV.	A Week Among the Utes	133
XVI.	Agriculture, Mining, Stock, and Climate	145
	Addenda	155

"Sierras, and eternal tents
Of snow, that flash o'er battlements
Of mountains."

A FORTNIGHT IN DENVER.

CHAPTER I.

A FORTNIGHT IN DENVER.

WE had come to Colorado to do the territory, and felt that we should not be satisfied with a casual glance either at any of the evidences of material prosperity in the cities, or Nature's wonderful manifestations in the "hill country." For, in the first place, we were tourists — not traveling to scatter money, live in the best hotels, and follow in the footsteps of fashionables or invalids; and, on the other hand, we all felt that, blessed in body, and endowed somewhat with appreciative minds for the beautiful in this life, we could spend a few weeks profitably, after a manner generally termed in the frontier dialect, roughing it. With a theoretical knowledge of Colorado, — as many others may have into whose hands this volume may fall, — we had long felt a desire growing within us to verify by experience the marvelous reports concerning this highly favored section of America, where, we had been told, Nature has placed her treasure vaults, and where the invalid can secure length of days, and the sight-seer ample recompense for his time and money. And this is why we — my friends and I — made up a party and traveled westward, over the plains, to the best known and most attractive of the territorial domain.

We remained in Denver perhaps a little longer than two weeks, making many friends amongst the cultured and hospitable people there, and storing up interesting facts relating to the foundation, growth, and development of this wonderful city. It is rightly termed a wonderful city; for where, even in this progressive and aggressive frontier — where cities are ofttimes builded in a year — can be found the same material evidences of healthful growth and well-grounded prosperity? In more than one respect it is a marvel of western pluck, having been created by the accident of gold discovery, and fostered through years of Indian troubles in the face of multitudinous discouragements. The finding of these auriferous deposits in the far western sands and rocks has been the means of opening up the avenue for a fast incoming empire of hardy people with pioneer instincts and adventuresomeness. We find it here, and everywhere in this sunset land.

It is not the intention of these pages to surfeit the reader with labored statistics concerning this city or the surrounding country, for the writer fully appreciates the terrible affliction of being pelted with books of travel crammed with figures that have no possible practical value, any more than would the multiplication table or strings of logarithms have been of use to Adam in the garden. Ignorance of board of trade reports, thermometrical observations on the weather, tabulated statements, and market valuation of real estate is bliss to the traveler, unless he be of that Gradgrindian temperament which yearns for facts and nothing else. There are a great many things to be told of in a plain way, which, I think, may not fail to interest even the man who wants to read as he runs.

Denver is a city of fifteen years' growth, and is to-day as stalwart and sinewy in her development, resources, and population as many a town of half a century's patient nursing. The nomadic characteristics of the people who came here in the early months of 1859 — and drifted here and there, just as the mining stampedes actuated — is no longer apparent, and the citizens chiefly are those who have come to stay, and are "growing up with the country," or, it might be said, are drawing the country up after them into an era of unexampled prosperity. The city presents an imposing appearance, as well after a protracted residence as upon first sight. It boasts of broad avenues lined with shade trees, of sightly and stately mansions, massive business blocks, and all the modern accessories that tend to make up a metropolitan city. From a log-and-canvas hamlet it has developed into a city of masonry, not equaled in the trans-Missouri country.

The city of Denver is built in an elliptical basin, tilted, so to speak, toward the mountains. The highest rim being toward the north and east, from that side of the city one obtains a view of mountain scenery such as the world nowhere else presents. The picturesque grouping of peaks and foot-hills, the undulating sweep of the snow-covered range,— the backbone of the continent,— the massive mountains as a whole, ever changing and yet the same, ever fresh in their gorgeous coloring, ever awful in their magnitude; all these are attractive features to a residence in this city. Standing like a sentinel over this army of mountain tops — hoary, snow-clad, and cloud-capped — eighty miles away from Denver, to the northwest, is Long's Peak, its summit 14,150 feet above the level of the sea. It stands boldly to the front, greeting the new-comer, and forming ever a picture upon which the eye never tires in dwelling. Long's Peak is one of the most difficult of ascent in the range. To the southwest we can distinctly see, apparently only a dozen miles removed, the historic mountain which once gave "a local habitation and a name" to all this section of the country — Pike's Peak. It is seventy-five miles to its base, as the bird flies, from Denver. And far beyond these giant mountains, north and south, the range sweeps away, until, on the one hand, it is lost in the Black Hills, north, and, on the other, in the Spanish Peaks and Sangre de Cristo mountains, south. There is a panoramic view of nearly three hundred miles of mountains, within the range of vision. You can sit in your room in Denver and take in this scene.

Advice, with regard to seeing a city, is cheap, both for the giver and receiver, and is treated by the latter much as cheap things generally are. It is of very little consequence to anybody except the one who kindly volunteers it.

Every person who travels has his own notions, and I will, therefore, offer but a few suggestions in a general way. The reader can use them as he sees fit. Strangers can spend a week in Denver, very profitably, viewing the city, riding about the suburbs, noting the wonderful improvements, asking questions as to the attractive mountain resorts, and arranging for a trip, which, to enjoy the life and get all the benefits of mountain touring, should be made by camping out, and avoiding hotels as much as possible. Denver has no ancient objects of interest; no antique gems of art; it is all an embodiment and manifestation of the new life of an enterprising people who pay more attention to money-getting than to æsthetics, and who will talk to you as enthusiastically of a new post-office, a suburban addition, or a three-story iron front, as will the Romans of their Sistine Chapel, or the Campagna, or the Milanese of their magnificent cathedral. In all this there is a freshness invigorating to a new-comer unfamiliar with western ways.

You will find, if you stay in Denver long enough, that the city has a strong claim on the summer travel, and that she looks longingly, every spring, to the season when the invalid, with his asthma, consumption, or general debility, shall turn hitherward from the miasmatic centers of the east, gain health, and lend renewed activity to the general business of the city; for the tourists and the invalids do give the city something of the appearance of the season at an eastern watering place.

Denver is growing with a rapidity unprecedented. Four years ago she had a population of five thousand; there are now nearly twenty thousand people who make their homes here. The limits of the city are continually extending; building is going on rapidly. Railroads reach from here to all parts of the territory, making the city a center, the development of which nothing will retard. By means of these thoroughfares Denver becomes the entrepôt for the whole territory, and by them all the resources of Colorado are tributary to Denver. With schools as well graded as any at the east; with a plentitude of churches; and with an able daily press, the mental and religious welfare of the citizens is guaranteed. In my opinion, Denver is destined to become a mammoth city — the only great city on the great plains. It will become the half-way station across the continent, which no tourist can pass without halting at.

The territory of Colorado, above nearly all other portions of the far western country, is replete with interesting resorts, as these pages show. The fastnesses of the mountains and the broad expanse of plains present attractive points toward which much of the tourist tide sweeps during the summer's solstitial heat, or the early season when nature "purples all the ground with vernal flowers." As the succeeding years drift by, and the wonders and beauties and oppressive grandeur of this famed section become better known; as tourists and health seekers spread the information they acquire; as means of transit are daily improved, and the heart of the continent is placed next door to the four quarters of the Union; so Colorado becomes more and more the objective point of pleasure seekers, and meets in every particular the roseate descriptions that her most enthusiastic admirers have written concerning her. Those who once obtain a glimpse of the mountains or partake of the health-giving and exhilarating air; who clamber over the rugged rocks or "loaf and invite their souls" in indolent leisure around the springs; who catch hurried glimpses of localities or tarry for weeks amongst nature's primitive abodes; all these instinctively turn back, as soon as opportunity offers, to enjoy again, to a fuller degree, if possible, the pleasure of former visits. Colorado is becoming the tourist's pivotal point. Tiring of the enervating influences of eastern watering places, palled with the fashionable frivolities of the beach and the insipid life of the shoddy centers of the east; with the beaten paths of summer travel offering no inducements for a respite from the cares of business life; the summer seekers of pleasure and recuperation turn their faces towards this western world, to visit new scenes, to live amongst a new people, to catch somewhat of the inspiriting genius of their life and activity, and to wonder always over the awful and impressive handiwork of nature which abounds on every side.

As Denver is the metropolitan center and business entrepôt of this territory, so also is it the diverging point from which the tourist turns to visit all sections of the territory. From this city the means of communication with the outside sections are perfect. The traveler who desires to visit the summer resorts of Colorado Springs, or the pleasant cities of far southern Colorado — Pueblo, Cañon, or Trinidad; who wishes to go into the mountains to Black Hawk or Central, the gold centers; to Idaho Springs, with her wonderful baths and beautiful cañons and peaks; to Georgetown or Caribou, the silver-producing districts; to Gray's Peak, Long's Peak, Pike's Peak or Mount Lincoln, the watch-towers of the continent; to the parks, with their wealth of mountain scenery, fish, game, mineral springs and rocky gorges; to Manitou, with her medicinal waters; to the marvelous rocks of the Garden of the Gods, or the disintegrated sandstone sentinels of Monument; whatever section it is desired to reach, Denver stands to it as the departure point.

The season being advanced — the month of July — when we made the pleasant sojourn here of which I now write, we cut short our stay in Denver and hastened to the mountains.

INTO THE AMERICAN SWITZERLAND.

C. C. R. R. CLEAR CREEK CAÑON.

J. COLLIER, PHOTO.

CHAPTER II.

INTO THE AMERICAN SWITZERLAND.

IN the ante-railroad days in these mountains, when staging was the only means of travel for the tourist, it used to be accounted a noteworthy trip to ride from Denver to Central City. The old road then crossed Guy Hill,— the chief point of interest on the route, — down which it zigzagged, and from the brow of which it was painful to gaze into the valley below, where sparkled a purling stream. It was the delight of the Jehus then, who held the reins over six fiery horses, to turn the first descent at break-neck speed, swinging the wheels of the coach dangerously near the precipice, and, by turning the leaders abruptly, cause the timid to cry out with fear at the impending prospect of a tumble over the rocks to the level below. This stage road ran high on the mountain sides, here and there, and at various elevations the open plains to the east and the snowy range to the west would present a panoramic view of the grandest description.

All is changed now, and the old wagon road is but little traveled. The railway coaches have again met the stages and crowded them from their former field of usefulness. The locomotive engine now wakes the echoes from the beetling rocks. This progressive age is abrogating all the rights the slow-coach era enjoyed. What was but two years ago the journey of a day, is now condensed to a few hours, and the ride down the dangerous hill roads and by the frowning precipices, has here given place to a trip through one of the most remarkable cañons accessible in the mountain region. It is here that the iron rails have been laid, over which the cars clamber up the mountains through a region where it would be supposed it were impossible to construct a railway. By the means of this road the mining districts are brought next door to Denver, transportation made easy and travel facilitated.

The Colorado Central Railway, which reaches from Denver into the mountains, passing through Clear Creek Cañon, makes a detour through a rich agricultural region on its route to Golden, the point where the grade changes from broad to narrow and the mountain ascent begins. This valley is considered one of the most attractive in the territory, and it certainly is entitled to the reputation if its products are any criterion upon which to base judgment. The fertile valley is dotted with thrifty farms, and the waving grain is an index of its farming facilities, when water can be applied to the soil.

Denver, Black Hawk and Floyd Hill are the termini of the Colorado Central, but the narrow-gauge portion, which

CLEAR CREEK CAÑON, C.C.R.R.

J. COLLIER, PHOTO.

extends through the cañon, reaches only from Golden, seventeen miles west of Denver, to the two other points mentioned. Of necessity there is a transfer at Golden, from the broad, large cars to the small, cosy little carriages, of the three-feet gauge, in which, it is facetiously said, the passenger must preserve his equilibrium with the utmost nicety. They are, however, safe and perfectly adapted to mountain railroads; in short, the only cars suitable for abrupt curves and heavy grades. For a short distance after leaving Golden the Colorado Central runs through an open country, at the base of the foot-hills, the grade of which constantly ascends, until, at last, the cars reach the narrow opening which constitutes the mouth of the cañon. Lofty foot-hills rise on either hand, covered with grass and dwarfed and scrubby pines, while the outcropping rocks, where huge fragments have been torn off to permit the little road to pass, would seem to threaten momentary danger to any object beneath. On the left, and far below the road-bed, Clear Creek — a stream now misnamed by reason of its dirty flood, made so by the numerous quartz mills in and about the gold region at Central and Black Hawk — dashes and foams in its hurry to join the Platte River far off on the plains. On the hill-side, above the creek, winds an irrigation flume which heads up in the cañon, and through which water is carried to the farms in the valley below.

The little engine which draws the train up this steep incline pants and groans, and the cars creak and twist and shake as in the throes of some great agony. On and on along the water-course the little road extends, until, a few more miles passed, the track and the creek draw near together, and the remainder of the distance lies within a few feet of the water. Now, the curving and the twisting of the track becomes more frequent, and the towering mountains shut out the plains behind. Vegetation changes, and the mountain sides are covered with pines from their summits to the water level. Bleak rocks stand out over the road and over the creek, assuming fantastic shapes; huge boulders, torn from the mountain sides by the engineers who piloted this little road up here, dam up the creek at various points. The track twists and turns and dodges into seemingly impassable openings, steadily climbing the mountains at the average grade of one hundred and seventy feet to every mile. The frowning rocks grow more terribly sublime, their height increasing, until, from the narrow defile, and out of the car window, it strains the eye to scale their tops. Now and then the mountain walls sink back and open out a stretch of meadow land, but soon again they hem the railroad in and the tortuous windings continue.

There is a station away up in the cañon, named Beaver, where the little engines always halt as though to recuperate and gather strength for the long strong pull up the remainder of the journey. It is one of the most romantic spots on the trip. Up the road there is a broad bold sweep of curve that seemingly carries the track into the heart of the granite pile;

below, the road is lost only a short distance away under the beetling crags; the only evidence of habitation is the station-house, and one or two other slight edifices. Perched high up on the rocks above the station-house is a pavilion reached by a long staircase. It hangs like an eyrie from a cleft in the rocks. It is to this place that pleasure parties make moonlight excursions from the valley and the mountain cities during the summer season. It is a charming retreat. A mountain rivulet comes down the breezy gulch above the station, and empties into Clear Creek. They who live at Beaver Creek, will tell you how, one summer night not long ago, a storm cloud burst in the gulch above, and how the watery wall swept everything before it as it rushed on its way to the main stream. It took with it the station-house, the water-tank, and everything else, and the frightened men who were sleeping there escaped with their lives only. These storms, however, are not of frequent occurrence. Fragrant flowers and beautiful ferns abound here, growing in the crevices of the rocks, and up and down the Beaver gulch.

This is a road of short tangents and innumerable curves. The route is more winding than a snake track. Straight track is almost unknown. It is a marvel of engineering skill. Its bed is as firm as the very mountains themselves, being laid upon the rocks. The bridges are securely built, and the whole safe for travel.

Some distance above Beaver Creek, the north and the south forks of Clear Creek unite, and here the road branches, one line reaching to Black Hawk, and the other over towards

Idaho Springs, the great summer resort of this region. The route to Black Hawk opens up a new country, the mountains dwindling into hills, the rocks giving way to narrow strips of tillable land. First glimpses of gulch mining are here obtained, for the bed of the creek has been washed and rewashed for its auriferous deposits. Along its length stretch narrow flume boxes, through which the dirty stream rushes. The sand has been worked for miles, and little beside the boulders have been left. The road passes the mouth of a tunnel which a company purpose driving twelve miles through the mountain bases until it shall reach Middle Park. We will find up here, also, that the biased-eyed Celestial has made his advent, and that his cheap labor is making gulch mining profitable. There is a Chinese settlement, just below Black Hawk, the members of which are working under lease from a white firm. They live quietly, are industrious and frugal, and have done very well in these placers. Upon the outskirts of Black Hawk the road enters a gulch filled with sulphurous vapors, highly suggestive of the infernal regions. These are from the works where gold ores are roasted and the separation of precious and base metals made. Then, with a strong pull up a heavy grade, the miniature train is lifted into the Black Hawk depot, a depot which cost one hundred thousand dollars, through the reckless expenditure of a once noted general and worthless miner, Fitz John Porter. It was erected as a quartz mill. From the Black Hawk depot to the heart of Central City is only a mile, the two towns joining each other.

The branch of the Colorado Central that we left at the junction of the forks, is pointing towards Georgetown. This branch of Clear Creek, unsullied by the refuse of quartz mills, is a noble stream, rapid and clear. The scenery along this route is superior to that of the other fork of Clear Creek, the rocks being grander and more massive, the windings and twistings more intricate. It finally emerges at the foot of Floyd hill, over which the old stage road runs. The ride from the terminus to Idaho Springs is a rich experience, the distance being very short and the country wonderfully beautiful.

It is a common thing to term this Clear Creek cañon the Yosemite of Colorado. While its scenery is not so massive as that of the great valley of California, it has beauties equally as attractive. The railroad now places it within the reach of everybody who visits the Territory, no matter how short may be his time for observation. Its natural characteristic is that of a cleft in the rocks, made by some volcanic action, with walls on either side, and towering mountains back of them thousands of feet above the little creek which dances and foams and roars over the rocks at their base. A ride up the cañon and back will convince any person that the mountain range was never created that man cannot cross with a locomotive engine.

A WEEK IN THE GOLD REGION.

CHAPTER III.

A WEEK IN THE GOLD REGION.

IT has been facetiously remarked by some traveled person, that one short leg is necessary to get about Central City and Black Hawk with any facility — that is, that the hillsides are so steep that pedestrianism is only made easy by a discrepancy in the length of limbs. There isn't enough level ground in these two cities to accommodate a circus tent, and it was the current joke of newspapers last summer, that the reason a menagerie never visited Central City was because of the impossibility to get the elephant through Clear Creek cañon, and of the absence of level ground here on which to pitch the canvas. But the rugged, rocky, uneven surface has been the cause of the building up here of a thriving settlement by hardy, earnest, ambitious men.

The gold discoveries in Clear Creek, in 1859, near to Denver, led the pioneer prospectors to try new fields, in the hope of discovering greater riches than were even dreamed to exist in these mountains. One earnest man toiled up the creek, to a point near where this city now stands, and made the discovery which has rendered his name noteworthy. The Gregory lode, now a remarkable mine, was named in honor of this prospector. With his friends, new and rich discoveries were made, and it was not long before these gulches, right and left, were filled up and overflowing with a restless, striving, ambitious and greedy army of men, who, drawn from the States by the wonderful reports of gold discoveries, had come out to try their luck and seek their fortunes in this new and comparatively unknown land. The settlement was but the outgrowth of the mining excitement at first. These cities, then, were nothing more than collections of rude log huts, and coney holes in the rocks. Everything was irregular and residence uncertain. The greater portion of those who came, without a cent to their names, were content to realize a few thousands in dust and then leave the country for ever. And so these cities grew up; new discoveries were continually making, the refractory character of ores necessitating the employment of improved machinery; until at last, after a few years, the cities became established facts, and grew into pretentious centers. To-day there are between 6,000 and 7,000 inhabitants in Central City and Black Hawk. The cities are so close together that it is impossible for a citizen of one to tell where he lives without going out of doors and looking at some landmark.

Central City and Black Hawk are built on auriferous foundations, and it is a point the local papers delight in making, for the astonishment of eastern readers, that the stone houses are made of gold-bearing quartz, and that ex-

cavations frequently yield enough of the precious metal to more than recompense the labor. These are some of the advantages of a habitation in this section.

Central City and Black Hawk give the new-comer the idea that the towns might, at some former day, have been located on the mountain top, and that some convulsion of nature had slid them pell mell into the gulch. The streets are irregular in shape, their general direction being more the result of mine development than any original plan on the part of the founders to lay out any thing like a comely city. The road that carries us up the gulch, and through the two cities, from the Black Hawk depot, runs, a portion of the way, along the side of Bobtail Mountain, like a notch cut for a passage way. Below, on the right, is muddy Clear Creek. Across the gulch, and up and down the mountain, are dwellings, and shapely school houses, and handsome churches, in seemingly unapproachable places. Long staircases reach from streets below to houses above, which, like Babylon of old, have their hanging gardens that seem to threaten the pedestrian underneath with instant destruction. Here and there the sombre shaft houses reach like stepping stones along the lode to the top of the hill, and, below, the ponderous machinery of the stamp mills beats and crushes the rich rock which yields in turn the auriferous standard of worldly value. Dark and dank tunnels gape upon this little world, by the road sides, and lumbering wagons go here and there with tinkling bells, drawing quartz to the mills. Everything betokens the industry of the district.

The mountains are spotted with dump piles and prospect holes, and seamed with rich mineral. The people are a mining people, earning their worldly wealth, for the most part, by delving in the bowels of the earth.

There are several things that will attract the attention of every person of an enquiring mind who comes to this place. One of these is the abundance of children, and another thing their apparent healthfulness. Nowhere in the country do we see such rugged, hearty, bronzed, and muscular children as in the Rocky Mountains, and nowhere in the mountains do you find more of them than here. They are pictures of health. Mountain air, the exercise of climbing the steep roads and running over the rocks, harden their physical natures and make them tough and sinewy. This is also a characteristic of older people. The young ladies are ruddy and healthy; the men muscular and hardy. A residence of a few weeks or months at Central City is sure to tone up any shattered system, give the spirits greater buoyancy, increase the circulation of blood and improve the general health. Sheltered in the gulch, the winds are not strong, with rare exceptions, and the temperature is remarkably equable.

Mining operations are comparatively little understood by the majority of the traveling public. They do not know the difference between gulch and lode mining, could not tell a sluice box from a furnace, and are perfectly at sea on the definitions of back-stoping and drifting. As for the characteristics of quartz, they invariably insist that iron pyrites is pure gold, and pronounce rock worthless if the auriferous deposit does not show to the naked eye. Stamp mills are, to them, but so many machines for breaking up quartz and losing all the gold, while separation of base bullion from the precious metal is a mystery that passes all comprehension. The tourist in the Rocky Mountains should improve the opportunity that is here afforded to inform himself on these varied terms and multiform operations. There is no better place to receive education on these points than right here in Central City and Black Hawk. There are gulch mines down the creek, there are deep shafts or lodes working here, there are stamp mills and concentration and separation works, and more than all these, there are here miners who know their calling perfectly, and who are never so well pleased as when imparting information to those who sincerely ask it. Several days may be profitably spent in visiting these gold mines, and storing knowledge of the technical terms and operations and the bullion yield of the country.

It is customary for those who come to these cities to make excursions to James' Peak, up which there is a splendid wagon road, and from which a view can be obtained that will never be effaced from the memory. The road is, like many others we constantly travel up here, full of surprises in snow-covered peaks, beautiful watercourses, verdant gulches and shimmering lakes. It is ten miles from Central to the summit of the peak, and it can easily be made in three or four hours. As we passed over the road, the clouds in the distance betokened rain, and, before we reached our destination, a drenching storm caught us, and baptised us with cool, refreshing drops. It laid the dust in the road-way, as well, and made travel pleasanter, for it only lasted a short time. When the storm cloud had swept below us and enveloped the lower country in mist, the trees about us wore a greener tint; the aspens shook moisture upon the grass below and sparkled with renewed beauty; the flowers wore a fresher look, and lifted their fragrant heads as though imbued with new life; the rocks displayed their variegated hues and streaks; and the effulgent sunlight seemed intensified a thousand-fold.

James' Peak well sustains the reputation of being one of the highest mountains in this section, and yet it is so accessible that the journey to its summit may be made in any buggy over a road always kept in the best condition. From its summit, and from the path-way we travel as well, beautiful lakes may be seen far below, and wonderful rocks far across the intervening chasm. Miles away to the westward we can look down into Middle Park, and behold as well the circling range of mountains which encloses that charming retreat; to the northeast is Long's Peak; to the southwest stretching successions of dizzy heights and dark, inviting valleys. Far off, on the plains, we may see, on a clear day, the glittering windows and spires of Denver, the

J. COLLIER, PHOTO.

city itself focalized by the great distance into a miniature town.

We traveled down to the lower and more comfortable country, after feasting the eyes with the rich perspectives and foregrounds of the great picture that had been unrolled before us, and made our way back to the quarters which awaited us at the Teller House. We were filled with pleasing thoughts and touched with a feeling akin to awe as we descended from this mount which raises its head almost to the very heavens.

We left Central City with the feeling that the sojourn there had been one of profit to us all. We penetrated to the bottom of some of the deep mines — a journey that requires some courage; we investigated the various processes used for taking gold out of the rocks; we passed through the sulphurous regions of the concentration works; and came away with a theoretical knowledge, at least, of the operations of gold mining. Tourists who desire to see these things are afforded the opportunity. All they are obliged to do is to stop a few days here, ask questions, pedestrianize a good deal, and display a modicum of common sense.

TO ESTES' PARK AND UP LONG'S PEAK.

CHAPTER IV.

TO ESTES' PARK AND UP LONG'S PEAK.

THIRTY miles from Longmont, up the Valley of the St. Vrain, is Estes' Park, the point from which the ascent of Long's Peak is made. For a few miles the road is through an open country, over bluffs and into the foot-hills at the base of this great mountain. The road is easily traveled, and is laid in the midst of mountain scenery which, while it may not have the stupendous grandeur of some other sections of which I have before written, is possessed of a quiet charm that makes the journey noteworthy in every respect. We came up here well prepared for mountain life, with the object in view of devoting a week or more to trout fishing, hunting, and making the ascent of Long's Peak. There were scores of tourists who had preceded us on the same mission, but, while they had met with unparalleled luck in the two former, only a limited number had scaled the mountain. This little mountain park, similar in its natural contour to the more extensive areas of country which make up the grand park system of Colorado, is replete with grassy slopes, crystalline streams that course down from the melting snow banks, broad zones of pine forests, towering heights of mountains, and shady nooks. It is just such a resort as the sportsman delights in, or the tourists loves to frequent. The streams are filled with trout, the pines abound with noble game.

The ascent of Long's Peak is no pleasure excursion, when viewed in the light of the exertion necessary to scale its summit. It is a forbidding height, the trail is a tedious one, but the reward in the magnificent view that crowns the labor of the climbing, more than repays the fatigue and exhaustion. For some distance after leaving the park, which presents the only accessible trail up this mountain, the ascent is comparatively an easy one, but soon the route becomes filled with seemingly insurmountable barriers, flanked by yawning chasms, and apparently blocked with impenetrable walls. Over rough and jagged boulders, along the edge of shelving rocks, in the light air that makes breathing difficult, and nearly prostrates the physical energies, up and up the way leads us, until, at last, we reach the very summit with only the blue sky above us, fleecy clouds breaking against the mountain side below, and half the continent seemingly spread out beneath our feet.

I can do no better here than quote the words which a lady has written descriptive of the ascent of this peak. They form a pen-picture of rare beauty, and are strikingly comprehensive. After leaving the park, and having traveled a portion of the route, she concludes the journey as follows:

"The trees grew smaller and more sparse as we ascended, and had a rugged, tortured, warring look, until the timber line was passed. But, a little higher, a slope of mountain meadow dipped to the southwest, towards a bright stream forcing its way through ice and icicles, and there a grove of the beautiful balsam pine marked our camping ground. The trees were in miniature, but so exquisitely arranged that one might well ask what artist's hand had planted them, scattering them here, clumping them there, and training their slim spires toward heaven.

"Looking east, gorges opened to the far distant plains, then deepening into purple gray. Mountains mantled with dark pines rose in ranges, or, solitary, lifted their bald, gray peaks; while, close behind, and nearly 4,000 feet above us, rose the splintered summit of Long's Peak, snow here and there upon its rugged wall, and its huge precipices red with the light of a sun already lost to our vision. Close to us, in the cavern side of the mountain, was snow that, owing to its position, is eternal, forming the frigid, ghastly background of the scene.

"The dawn seemed so long before sunrise, so lemon-colored, so pure; and the sunrise itself was a never-to-be-forgotten sight. From the chill gray peak above, from the everlasting snows, from the silvered pines—down through mountain ranges with their depths of Tyrian purple, we looked to where the plains lay cold in the blue-gray, like a morning sea against the verge of the far horizon. The sun rose above the cold gray line, a dazzling streak at first, then an enlarging portion of a sphere, a light and glory as when it first appeared in the firmament. I felt as if, like a Parsee, I must fall down and worship. The gray of the plains changed to purple, the sky was all one crimson flush on which vermilion cloud-streaks rested, the ghastly peaks gleamed like rubies, the earth and heavens were new created. For a full hour those plains simulated the ocean, down to whose limitless expanse of purple, cliffs and rocks and promontories swept down.

"Passing through the 'Notch,' we looked along the inaccessible side of the peak, composed of boulders and *débris* of all shapes and sizes, through which appeared broad, smooth ribs of reddish-colored granite, looking as if they upheld the towering rock-mass above.

"Here the very business of the ascent begins, and it would not be very easy to overestimate its difficulty and fatigue. Two thousand feet of solid rock towered above us; two thousand feet of broken rock shelved precipitous below; smooth granite ribs with hardly foot-hold stood out here and there; melted snow, re-frozen several times, presented a more serious obstacle; many of the rocks were loose and tumbled down the slope when touched; and to me it was four hours of extreme terror. Indeed, I never should have gone half way, had not 'Jim,' *nolens volens*, dragged me along with a patience and skill, and withal a determination that I should ascend the peak, which never failed. After what seemed to me an exhausting amount of toil, we reached the real heavy grade of the ascent, a long gulch with inaccessible sides. This was partly filled with ice and snow, and partly with large and small fragments of rock which are constantly giving way, rendering the footing very insecure. Slipping, faltering, trembling from the hard toil in the rarefied air; with throbbing hearts and bursting lungs, we reached the top of the gorge, where a difficult climb between some gigantic fragments of rock introduced us, by an abrupt turn, round the southwest angle of the peak, to a narrow shelf several hundred feet long, rugged, uneven, and so overhung by the cliff in some places, that it is necessary to crouch to pass at all. Above, the peak is nearly vertical for about 500 feet, and below, a tremendous precipice descends in one unbroken fall. This is usually considered the most dangerous part of the ascent, but it does not seem so to me, for such foot-hold as there is, is secure, and it is generally possible to hold on with the hands. But here and on the final, and as I think, the worst part of the ascent, one slip, and a breathing, thinking human being would lie a shapeless, bloody heap, three thousand feet below.

"From hence the view, though different, is as magnificent as that from the 'Notch.' At the foot of the stupendous precipice lay a lovely lake, wood-embosomed, from or near which the bright St. Vrain takes its rise. Snowy ranges, one behind another, extended to the distant horizon, folding in their wintry embrace the beauties of Middle Park. Pike's Peak, more than a hundred miles away, lifted that vast but shapeless summit, which makes it the land-mark of southern Colorado. Giants everywhere reared their lonely splintered summits. There were snow-patches, snow-slashes, snow-abysses, snow forlorn and soiled looking, snow pure and glistening, snow dazzling above the purple robe of pines worn by all the mountains, while away to the east in limitless breadth stretched the green-gray of the endless plains. From hence with a single sweep the eye takes in a distance of three hundred miles — that distance to the west, north and south, being made up of mountains, ten, eleven, twelve, thirteen thousand feet in height, dominated by Long's Peak, Pike's Peak, Gray's Peak, all nearly the height of Mt. Blanc! On the plains, we traced the rivers by their fringe of cottonwoods to the distant Platte, and, between us and them, lay glories of mountain, cañon and lake, sleeping in depths of blue and purple most ravishing to the eye.

"The worst was yet to come. As we crept from the ledge round a horn of rock, I beheld what made me perfectly dizzy to look at — the terminal peak itself, a smooth, cracked face or wall of pink granite, as nearly perpendicular as anything could be, up which it was impossible to climb, well deserving the name of the 'American Mätterhorn.' Scaling, not climbing, is the correct term for this last ascent. It took one hour to ascend that five hundred feet, stopping every four or five steps to get breath. The only foothold was in narrow cracks, or on minute projections on the granite. To get a toe in these cracks, and on hands and knees to crawl, to be dragged up by main force, to get hold here and there on a scarcely obvious projection, all the while gasping and struggling for breath, and tortured by thirst — this was the climb; but at last the peak was won.

"A grand, well-defined mountain top it is — two or three acres of boulders, nearly level, with precipitous sides all round, the one we came up being the only accessible one.

"Here were seen, in one unrivaled combination, all the views which had rejoiced our eyes during the ascent. It was something, at last, to rest upon the storm-rent crown of this lonely sentinel of the Rocky Range, on one of the mightiest of the vertebræ of the back-bone of this vast continent, and to see the waters start for both oceans. Uplifted beyond war, and hate, and storms of passion; calm amidst the eternal silence; fanned by zephyrs, and bathed in living blue, Peace seemed to rest upon the peak, as if it were indeed that region

"'Where falls not rain, or hail, or any snow,
  Or ever wind blows loudly.'

"We placed our names, with date of ascent, in a tin within a cairn, and afterward accomplished the slippery and perilous descent in safety, remaining that night at the camping ground owing to excessive fatigue, and reaching

Evans' delightful ranche, in Estes' Park, at noon of the following day. A more successful ascent of the peak was never made, and I would not now exchange my memories of its perfect beauty and extraordinary sublimity for any other experience of mountaineering in any other part of the world."

BOULDER CANON.

BOULDER FALLS

J. COLLIER, PHOTO.

swirling and seething sheets tumbling down precipitous rocks and dashing with tremendous fury against buttressing arms of granite that reach half-way across the stream. Twelve miles of this road — a distance seemingly not half so great — and we are at the falls, or near thereto. These falls are on the North Boulder Creek, a few hundred yards above the point where that branch joins the Middle Boulder. A winding trail around the mountain side carries us to the falls, a sheet of water of beauty and considerable volume.

Now and then, in making the tour of Boulder Cañon, the eye can discern, far up on the beetling heights, the forms of mountain sheep, which frequent these hills, and, like the chamois of the Alps, nimbly skip from crag to crag. Beyond the reach of deadly gun and hostile man, they gaze complacently down upon the tourist, who thus unceremoniously intrude themselves, in search of nature's wondrous works, upon their rightful domain. They clamber about on the ledges as securely as though they were on some broad plateau, and make safe leaps across the yawning chasms that would chill the blood of any acrobat. Their flesh is excellent for food, and the massive horns which adorn their heads are considered prizes by those who fancy taxidermic collections.

There is a growing settlement farther up, called Middle Boulder, or Nederland, in honor of the Caribou Mining Company, and beyond is the Caribou mine itself, in the heart of a large district of silver lodes which are the great resort in northern Colorado, and should never be slighted for any other attraction that may present itself. It lies on the route to other interesting localities, and is like a beautiful chapter in the complete volume of Colorado summer resorts. Through it the tourist may go either to Middle Park, to Central City, and thence to Georgetown, or to the hundred other places, less famous, perhaps, but equally interesting.

It is but a short distance from Boulder City to the point where the roadway enters the mountains, close to the creek, and begins its tortuous ascent amongst the rough and ragged rocks round which the river runs. The grade is an easy one, and travel very pleasant. In the early morning, when the sombre rocks were tinged with the bright sunshine that flooded the eastern plains, the keen air from the distant hill-tops and cool recesses bringing color to the face and reviving activity and elasticity in every muscle, we began the ascent. For miles the road winds in and out, across primitive bridges, and on and up the magnificent rocky opening. Each turn brings to light new views, rivaling all others passed in picturesque groupings and effects. It would seem that here is the studio of nature, where scenes that far excel all works of man's pencil are hung with lavish profusion upon the granite walls. Above, the towering heights seem piercing the very heavens, and down their sides the emerald foliage stands out in rich contrast with the back-ground. Below, the rushing creek boils and roars as it leaps from boulder to boulder, of this mountain region, which is by no means meagre. It is not a handsome city, but still has many characteristics of a lively, active, energetic commercial center. It is not large, the population not exceeding two thousand, yet it is composed, in the main, of that class of early settlers who, by their persistency, gave the place a habitation as well as name, and have seen it develop into a prosperous community. Five years ago there was little here beyond a cluster of insignificant dwellings, a few general stores, and several other of the accessories of a small town. But the people were hopeful. There was Denver, already grown to a thriving city, and Denver was securing eastern rail connections. The Boulderites knew that if this happened, their town would surely come in, some day, for a share of the general prosperity; and they were not disappointed.

Many Coloradans—and especially the residents in Boulder—think Boulder Cañon replete with the finest mountain scenery hereabouts. Opinions may differ on this point; but all are ready to concede that it is one of the most charming resorts readily reached from the cities principally visited. Its natural characteristics differ from those of Clear Creek Cañon, Cheyenne Cañon, or other accessible mountain resorts, displaying a more infinite variety of blending of rocks and dell, refreshing foliage and inviting gorges. The route up Cheyenne Cañon is by a trail, while here we can ride the entire distance in a wagon, and not suffer half the fatigue of the other trip. Boulder Cañon is

CHAPTER V.

BOULDER CANON.

DURING the mid-summer season it is a delightful ride from Denver to Boulder, either by the railroads which connect these cities — the Colorado Central and the Boulder Valley — or by the old wagon route which runs between the two and takes in more of the interlying agricultural region. The valleys of Clear Creek and Boulder are noted in this territory for the excellence of their soil, as well as rural picturesqueness. The farmers are prosperous, industrious men, who have done much to prove that the soil of Colorado has few equals for richness in the broad range of this Union. Irrigation ditches are seen on every knoll and hill-side where water can be carried, for it is the highest essential of a piece of land, in making a bargain, that the seller can say it is "under ditch." The distance to Boulder is about twenty-eight miles; but, as the road lies along the mountain base, and there is diversity of scenery to please the eye, one enjoys the trip, no matter how it is made.

The city of Boulder is situate at the opening of Boulder Cañon, and controls, to a great degree, the business

worked advantageously. The whole section is called Caribou, and there is no doubt but that it is one of the richest silver centers in the Rocky Mountains. It has grown into notoriety within five years. Its prosperity has been unchecked. The mine, from which the name for this point is taken, was sold two years ago for a sum approximating three millions of dollars, to a company formed in Holland. They are working it with great success. A mill is located near by in which the ore is treated and the precious mineral run into bullion, which makes it ready for the financial markets of the world. Mining is the one pursuit of this region. The lodes are situate far up on the mountain at an elevation of 9,167 feet. The embryogenic towns are filled with a rugged, hearty class of men who delve amongst the rocks and bring to light the treasures of the everlasting mountains. Gold Hill, another mining region, several miles away, between which and Caribou lies Sugar Loaf Mountain, is also thronged with persistent prospectors and lucky miners. There gold is obtained in quantities that seem almost incredulous when told.

It is about nineteen miles from Middle Boulder to Central, and the route is like many others in the mountains, precipitous but safe. The road winds through an attractive pass, where flowers blossom by the road-side and wild berries grow in profusion. On either side miniature cañons open wide their mouths, from which refreshing streams purl down the rocks. In the distance, the forests on the mountain sides grow hazy through the azure distance, and, further still, the snow-peaks stand out in all their glittering grandeur.

The traveler should occupy several days making the trip from Boulder to Central City, sauntering away the time in viewing the points of attraction. Trout fishing will also claim some attention of those given to this sport, for the creek is alive with these finny beauties. The distance of the round trip is about forty miles, but the journey is one which seldom offers itself to the traveler, and which, once enjoyed, will never be regretted.

It is the custom of those who have but limited time here to go through the Boulder Cañon, and over to Central, and thence back to Denver over the railroad, through Clear Creek Cañon. If one can spend no more time in Colorado than is essential to "do" these two points, they should be visited and the others neglected; but, in neglecting the others, the beauties, comforts and discomforts of mountain life are lost. This hurried, careless trip may be made by stage and cars in two days. By the easy stages of the sauntering tourist, double that time will be consumed.

IDAHO SPRINGS AND THE HOT BATHS.

CHAPTER VI.

IDAHO SPRINGS AND THE HOT BATHS.

THE most advantageous route to Idaho Springs is by way of Central City. There is one reason for this, if no more, and it is that the road lies over a beautiful country, far more attractive than that of the others. I say the country is beautiful; this is purely in the sense of its being mountainous. The distance to Idaho Springs would not be great, if we could drive in an air-line through the hills, but, as we are obliged to go, it is six miles, three of which are up a steep incline, and three down a cañon that has a pitch of about forty-five degrees. It is a long and severe pull up to the summit of Bald Mountain, which stands between Central and Idaho, and which it is necessary to scale to make the journey from the one place to the other. It is a tedious ride up the mountain side, the stage groaning and pounding and rolling, now pitching into the gullies, and again mounting some huge boulder.

We pass quartz mills and prospect holes, the latter dotting the hill-sides, and meet great wagons filled with crushed ore being hauled to the concentration works for treatment. There is a little town away up here that is called Nevada; but it is only a hamlet, with a sparse population and great mining prospects. Afar off, on a mountain side, beyond an intervening gulch, we behold a farm, the first met with at this altitude, the crops, apparently, growing thriftily nine thousand feet above the sea, and yielding good returns to the energetic husbandman. Central City from here, as we look back across our road just traveled, appears like a town jammed helter-skelter down into a gulch — set on edge — the houses apparently resting on each other's roofs, and suggesting momentarily a slide of the whole town down into the muddy but meagre stream. In traveling on, we rise nearer to the summit, until at last we stand upon a rocky plateau, amongst the aspen and the straggling and scrubby pines. Opening wide below us is Virginia Cañon, down which the road-way meanders, and which debouches at its foot, into the green and fertile Clear Creek Valley. Buttressing the cañon, but several miles away, is the hoary head of the "Old Chief," a mountain of some pretentions, and to which pleasure parties make excursions from Idaho Springs.

After reaching the brow of the hill, where begins the road down Virginia Cañon, we turn aside for a brief trip to an interesting point, which is less than a half mile from the main route to Idaho Springs. This spot is called Bellevue, and is at the edge of a towering hill, from which the snowy range may be viewed for miles

IDAHO SPRINGS AND THE HOT BATHS. 59

north and south. The far-away mountains here seem to sweep in the form of a semicircle, hemming in this point of observation and all the intervening and lower mountains away down to the plains. Below us we find delightful valleys, and on either hand far-reaching distances which are only met by the grand and gigantic range. With time at command, and traveling facilities which will permit of this short excursion, every tourist should turn aside, before beginning the descent of the cañon, and view the mountain scenery from the commanding height of Bellevue.

This roadway down Virginia Cañon is about three miles in length, and that entire distance it winds along the mountain side at the left. It is wide enough for a single vehicle, but turning-out places are made at regular intervals to provide for safety and prevent retracing steps should two teams meet, as is often the case. In going down, the left side of the road is met by the towering mountain wall, while to the right there is a yawning abyss hundreds of feet to the bottom. The road runs close to the edge of the precipice. If on a stage, the traveler should ride outside here, as everywhere, if possible, that he may take in the beauties of the scene. Some of the drivers delight in going down these hills at break-neck speed, and the favorite piece of mountain road for this pastime has been Virginia Cañon. It is the best plan to put your faith in the man who holds the reins, clutch tightly the guards around the box-seat, and begin the descent with the satisfied air of one enjoying the happiest moments of his life. Fear should not mar the delights of this ride, for, although the road does wind about the abutting rocks, and is lost here and there to view until the sudden turn is made that reveals it again for a few rods ahead, the gulch looks forbidding and suggestive of tumbles; although the fast revolving wheels slip suggestively toward the brink as the coach turns and obeys the guidance of the calm driver; with all these things, and the rolling and the pitching of the vehicle, there is no danger. Accidents do not happen here. The distance down, as I before stated, is about three miles — the descent perpendicularly more than two thousand feet. It is ofttimes made in eleven minutes. At the foot of the cañon we emerge into the narrow, yet inviting, valley of Clear Creek, turn the corner of the road sharply, and find ourselves, the next moment, in a compact little town, and driving up its principal street at a tearing gait. This is Idaho Springs.

It is a pleasing conceit of Coloradans that Idaho Springs is its chief watering place, by reason of its accessibility, romantic surroundings, and splendid and unsurpassed facilities for bathing. During the summer season the little town is overrun with tourists who divide their time between daily trips into the surrounding country, sporting in the exhilarating hot soda-water at Montague's Ocean Swimming Bath house, and living a fashionable life at the hotels. Days and weeks of unalloyed happiness may here be spent, with new scenes constantly presenting themselves, new faces daily arriving, and fresh surprises perpetually enjoyed. It is, in every sense, a gay, yet retired, retreat, where the devotee of pleasure, the admirer of nature, or the debilitated invalid may enjoy himself or find relief for the thousand ills which this weak flesh is heir to. The hot soda baths, for which this place is noted far and near, are given, as the bather may desire — either at the natural heat of the water, as it bubbles from the ground, or at a higher temperature. There is a fine bathing establishment in a cosy and inviting gulch within a short walking distance of the hotels, and to this the tourist or the invalid is sure to find his way at all hours of the day. Two large rooms are for swimming, and there both sexes join in the aqueous sports, clad in elegant bathing dresses. Those who desire may enjoy private baths in separate compartments. The water is ever fresh and healthful, continually passing in and out. It is clear and warm, and its mineral properties are such as to make it eagerly sought by all who visit this section.

There are delightful resorts close at hand, where all who wish may spend hours of pleasure. Winding trails lead to the summits of adjacent mountains, over to Chicago Lakes, up to the silver mines high on the hill-sides, to Fall River, and elsewhere. With delightful days come the invigorating nights, cool and refreshing. Nestled in the deep gorge, flanked by frowning and enchanting mountains, the little town, which boasts its thousand people, is a spot rarely equaled for attractive interest. As yet, the railroad does not reach it, but this only renders it more inviting and gives to it an air of rural surroundings that could scarcely be otherwise enjoyed. Up Clear Creek, west, the road leads to Georgetown; down the creek, east, to the railroad connection at the foot of Floyd Hill. The tide of travel through this place, in the season, is remarkable, the coaches being daily filled with tourists, and the road dotted both with pedestrians and other pleasure-seekers journeying with their own conveyances.

Idaho Springs is continually developing in interest and material prosperity. From the days when the sand-bars in Chicago Creek were washed for gold by the adventurous prospectors who came here in the early stampede, to the present, it has known prosperity. It is now a summer resort, and will so continue. The influx of easterners, and the increase of business, have established a handsome mountain town. Its people are enterprising and hospitable. After enjoying its society, its mountain scenery, and, more than all, its luxurious baths, I can only say, in my feeble way, that it has no superior in the mountains. With renewed vigor, from long tramps and rides up and down the mountains, and a prolonged season of hot baths, we left Idaho Springs only with regret, but still fully determined to renew our pleasant acquaintances and delightful experiences.

TO GEORGETOWN AND VICINITY.

CHAPTER VII.

TO GEORGETOWN AND VICINITY.

A DELIGHTFUL experience of the trip from Idaho Springs to Georgetown is the ride on one of the stage coaches which regularly ply between these points. The road is level and even, the greater portion of the distance bordering the bank of Clear Creek, which here is a stream of some size and much beauty. It was in the afternoon of one of those perfect days which here prevail — a day when the sky was unmarked by a single cloud, and a flood of golden sunshine filled the valleys and covered the mountain tops — that we began the journey to the city which lies in the very heart of one of the richest silver districts of Colorado. We took pains to secure seats on the top of the lumbering, rolling stage, that we might the better view the magnificent scenery and revel in the invigorating and refreshing air. With a driver who had traversed the mountain roads since the pioneer days of staging in this country; a fellow of infinite jest, and one whose judgment of human nature was infallible; who could make the pimples of fear creep over the body of a timid traveler at the recital of bloody tales, the recounting of hair-breadth escapes from treacherous mountain roads, or the horrible carnivals of plains savages, or who would relate with modest pride his experiences with noted people who had ridden under his guidance, far and near; with this reinsman, who, it was conceded, had no equal, we passed an afternoon of genuine pleasure and profit. His knowledge of the country through which we were traveling was perfect, and his conversation ready and intelligent, from questions of political economy to the far more practical topics of breaking leading horses or mending a disabled whiffletree. He had delved in the mines, had sluiced on the bars of the creeks, had run a country store, been road commissioner, and, in his younger days, had taught a district school, and, once on a time, even essayed the editorship of a country newspaper. We drew out of him the fact that he had once been a prospective millionaire,— in mines,— and that he still aspired to a position which, while it might not be half as dignified as stage-driving, would reap him rich financial advantages.

These men, or many of them, at least, who crack the whip from the top of a stage, and handle with dexterity six prancing horses, are striking examples of the vicissitudes which are incident to their life. We hear of them, as we travel, in the most remarkable conditions and precarious situations. No one knows precisely, as he looks upon their weather-bronzed visages, whether he be riding with some unfortunate college graduate educated highly in modern and classic lore, or whether his lot has been cast for the time with some broken-down professional who came with the first tide of adventurers to this land, and has known all the peculiarities of frontier life and experienced its every phase of hardship. They are, at all events, cosmopolites, cultivated in the school of the world, refined even in their brusqueness, and polished beneath their rough exterior. In pelting sleet or driving rain, in windy weather and in bright sunshine, they are at their posts, always ready with a pleasant word for those who can understand their apparent uncouthness, or as silent as a sphynx to those who presume upon their station. A stage driver is a king upon his seat; he is as imperious and exacting as a monarch of the realm; he knows his route and favors his horses; he yields to no one but the owner of his line; he is always pleased to ride beside an interesting lady. He is a cyclopedia of useful information, and can tell a Munchausenish story with the most plausible air. He is a friend, if rightly cultivated, but an implacable enemy if imposed upon.

Fall River is a resort adjacent to Idaho Springs, where summering tourists may spend the time at their disposal most profitably. In the stream, from which the little station takes its name, are good trout, which may be had as the reward for a tramp up the cañon and over the hills. Clear Creek here seems to burst suddenly from a rocky chasm, the sides of which tower thousands of feet towards the empyrean. There is a strange freak of nature on the southern side of the gorge, high above us, which has been called the Old Man of the Mountains. It has the semblance of a human face, grotesque yet regular, and, from its rocky eyrie, seems looking down with calm majesty upon the pigmies who come and go and live in the fastnesses below.

The road up the creek lies close to the water's edge, and is filled with surprises for those who make the journey for the first time. Here and there are the evidences of man's persistent search for hidden treasure in the rocks, tunnels opening their mouths on either hand, and shaft holes gaping far up the mountain sides. As we near Georgetown, the mountain scenery grows more picturesque, and we catch, now and then, glimpses of far-off peaks upon whose sides lie the everlasting snows. Winding up one of these great hills is a roadway, which, we are told, leads to cities where it would seem impossible for man to live. We catch sight of travelers wending their way along this seemingly dangerous route, where, to make a misstep would precipitate horse and rider thousands of feet down into the valley. Before us opens a notch, and in the perspective of the picture rises a cone-shaped mountain. This overlooks the city of Georgetown, while to the right and left are the mountains which flank it on either side. Into this gap the road enters. After a short ride we are carried to the brow of an eminence from which we obtain the first sight of the beautiful mountain city. It is attractive by comparison with other towns built in this altitude. The lower portion of the city straggles over the level space between Republican and Democrat mountains, and has been laid out with little regard to regularity. Beyond, and near to Leavenworth Mountain, which blocks up the western end of the valley, the city is more densely populated and more comely in its arrangement. As a whole, however, it is sightly and substantial.

Georgetown is the outgrowth of mining industries. The mountains about the city are seamed with argentiferous deposits. It is a metropolitan mining camp. The rocks have been made to yield up their treasures, and the ingenuity of man has established here works to refine the base bullion. Silver ore is the staple product. We find it piled about the shaft-houses and corded in the concentration works. We stumble over huge specimens at the hotels and in the doorways of the business houses. We find anxious prospectors ogling rich quartz with powerful glasses, and hear them talk of wonderful discoveries, at their meals and over their billiards. Speculators rise on every side with the most marvelous bargains in mines, and litigants abound with tales of shrewd operations and swindling games that have been practiced upon them. Mining goods in miners' stores pall upon the sight.

The bustle and business of the city is suggestive of a grand system of mining operations. Bricks of silver bullion attest the richness of some of the lodes which are worked with great profit. Like all mining centers, Georgetown has had its alternate seasons of prosperity and depression, incident upon the operations in the silver mines. With cheap labor and cheap modes of separating the bullion from the ores, so that low-grade quartz may be worked with even a moderate profit to the mine-owner, her present and future prosperity seems assured.

We had heard, before our arrival in Georgetown, of the many objects of interest which lie contiguous to this place. From here the journey to the summit of Grey's Peak can be made, and return, in a day, although it is not advisable to attempt so great a distance and so severe climbing in so short a time, unless one is in a great hurry. Being pleasure-seekers, we took our time, and would recommend everybody else to do the same. There is such a thing as indecent and unsatisfactory haste. Parties at the hotels plan excursions to Chicago Lakes, by means of mountain trails and the sure locomotion of grotesque *burros* (jacks) which are employed here for the purpose of packing ores from the mines on the mountain sides to the valley. These trips are enjoyable and invigorating, but there are few things more ludicrous than the appearance of a party ready for starting or after they get well on their winding way. The *burros* are diminutive animals, wiser looking than a patriarch, as patient as Job, and more fitly the type of innocence than any bas-relief lamb that ever graced a tombstone. As for beauty, they do not stand high in the animal kingdom, neither are they celebrated for speed, but they are sure-footed and strong-backed, and, therefore, useful. Large parties of ladies and gentlemen make these trips, and all return — a little sore and way-worn perhaps — pleased with this rich experience in mountaineering. There being a project of this kind on foot when we reached Georgetown, we hastened to enter into it, and can speak by the card when we recommend it to all who may glance at these pages. The road, to be sure, was a weary one, twisting here and there, and making precipitous ascents and descents; there were impertinent branches of dead pines to tear the clothes and scratch the skin; there were slippery steeps, and much jolting, and a great deal of patience wasted on the precise mule; but, with all these things, there was more than a recompense of rich experience and a wealth of mountain scenery that one could not reap otherwise. Taking blankets and food and utensils along, the trip is prolonged to the second day. Ladies as well as gentlemen make it easily.

The Georgetowners call it two miles from their city to Green Lake, a beautiful sheet of water nestled in a depression in the mountain-top two thousand feet above the town. If one walks it, he will think it ten miles; if he rides in a carriage, he will come to the conclusion that they are the longest two miles man ever measured. Passing the inevitable toll-gate, the road zigzags up the gulch at an angle of nearly forty degrees. A portion of the way it is quite well worn, but, as we pass the mines which are worked up here, the road becomes lost amongst small rocks and tree stumps, until it seems as though a vehicle could proceed no farther. But the driver, who knows the way, whips up his four horses, and, with many a pungent interjection, makes his way towards the destination. We are going up more than two thousand feet on an incline of two miles. The precipitous nature of the road may be estimated from this. Rich and fragrant flowers abound profusely, of all colors. The openings in the mountains disclose peak upon peak,— "Pelion on Osso piled,"— snow-capped and pine-clad. After a long, strong and earnest pull up the last grade, we come upon the little lake, a half mile long and less than a quarter mile wide. It glistens in the sunlight through the clustering pines, in the midst of which, upon the shore where we have emerged, stands a rude house owned by the young man who keeps the boats and rows visitors over the waters.

This lake is an emerald gem set in the mountain crown. Its waters appear, at first sight, to be of a dark green color, but they are as clear as a crystal. The eye can penetrate to a depth of eighty feet, and distinguish plainly the great rocks upon the bottom.

On one side pine trees are seen standing upright, presenting the appearance of having grown under the water. Echoes are superb, the sound reverberating from crag to crag, a dozen times, until it is lost to the ear. The lake water is ice-cold.

The peculiar green color given it is from coppery sediment on the rocks at the bottom. The lake was probably formed by a landslide, in the ages past, at the lower end of the gorge where the houses are built. There are boats at hand by means of which visitors can reach all the points of interest hereabouts. This lake is more than 12,000 feet above the sea level, and is one of the most noted in the mountains.

The ride down the steep road is quickly made, there being some sudden frights for timid people, here and there, but there is no danger, as the man at the reins knows his business and the route, and is sure to land his living freight safe at the hotel door.

SAUNTERING IN MIDDLE PARK.

THE CRATER-N.E. CORNER MIDDLE PARK.

J. COLLIER, PHOTO.

CHAPTER VIII.

SAUNTERING IN MIDDLE PARK.

GOING into the mountains without going over them to the parks that lie beyond, is to lose much of the pleasure of mountaineering. I look back upon the time spent in Middle Park as of the most enjoyable of the summer trip. Delightful days may be spent here in this, one of the great fertile areas where "majestic hill and plain seem wedded," where summer and winter unite, and where fecund life and barren rock are joined. It is a little paradise dropped amongst the mountains, where all is peace and quiet, where nature revels in her wildest moods, and where civilizing influences are only just beginning to make themselves felt. In the years past there were so many difficulties attending a journey to this point; nature had thrown up such seemingly impassable barriers, as if forbidding the approach of man and determined to reserve this spot for the natives of the streams and forest; the mountains were so high and the trails so treacherous, that people were deterred from going in, preferring to take the accessible points near at hand. By doing this, much of the finest scenery to be met with in these everlasting hills was lost.

No obstacles impede the progress of this generation. No mountain so high but man will devise some easy plan to cross it. No undertaking is too great for his accomplishment. Aware of the beautiful land beyond the dividing range, man has gone in to possess it and to utilize its resources. His energy has smoothed the rugged pathways and made communication with the regions across the snowy range a matter of comparative ease. More than forty of the ninety miles that lie between Denver and the hot sulphur springs, in Middle Park, can be made by cars and stage. This takes us to Georgetown, and from that point the road winds up the mountain sides and can be made on horseback, which, after all, is the preferable mode for mountain travel.

From Georgetown to the summit of the range, by the way of the Berthoud Pass, is a trip that unfolds an expanse of mountain scenery lovely beyond description. From bench to bench of mountain levels the trail ascends, here rough and rugged, steep and slippery, there smooth or undulating. Up, up, up the journey leads, more than 11,000 feet above the sea; the air the while growing more and more rarified and breathing becoming more and more difficult. The vegetation dwindles, the barren rocks stand out, and, on the summit of the range, we are lifted as it were into the very heavens. Here the waters of two oceans divide and course their way in opposite directions to the foaming streams in the valleys below; to the right and to the left, far away, the snow-slashed and chasm-rent mountains lift their heads in majestic grandeur; the sweeping winds carry the fleecy clouds far above our heads and down the mountain sides below our feet; awful abysses yawn before us and behind us; above, the beetling crags look contemptuously down upon our puny forms, made more insignificant by this massing of nature's giant forces; the towering pines on the hill-sides, beyond, dwindle to the size of currant bushes; while all around there is the manifest presence of the Great Master who fashioned these hills and who holds the world in the hollow of his hand. Here, the effulgent sunlight beams upon us and makes the scene one of grandeur more sublime than nature in her most charming form can elsewhere present. There, away across the mountain tops, the clouds hang heavy and dark and the elements do battle. In the valleys, sunshine chases shadow a merry race across the rocks, and the clouds, with all the fickleness of maiden's love, are gay and sad by turns. It were worth a journey of half the globe to stand up here above the world and look upon these scenes.

The objective point of the tourist who goes to Middle Park, is Hot Sulphur Springs, a bathing place made by nature, where a stream of hot water, 110° Fahrenheit, falls over a ledge of rock, and in which the invalid may find relief from all manner of maladies. Dense forests are passed on the road down from the summit, and stretching plateaus are traversed, and brooks crossed which abound with trout, and the Fraser River met, a stream angry and rapid. There are a few buildings at the springs, rough houses, but it is thought a respectable sized town will be built up there. The Grand River flows through the park here, and the hot springs are near its bank. We pitched our tents in this vicinity and made the springs the base of our perambulations and excursions.

It is not an easy task to convey by the means of cold words and expressionless paper an adequate idea of the experiences developed by a journey over these mountains and into the spacious yet cosy plain hemmed in on every side. Experience is the only true guide and teacher in such matters. One must see for himself; others' eyes are poor media in a case of this kind. Printed pages give but an inkling of the beauties written of, like the dim outline of some gorgeous landscape from which an obscuring fog lifts for a moment only to settle down the next and shut the scene in more closely. During our little lifetime of rural joy — compressed into a week — which we spent here, we passed the days in a round of excitement with fresh scenes and new pleasures constantly arising. The river was covered with water-fowls, comparatively tame, so little had they been hunted, and above and below the springs — according to the frequency of fishermen's visits — trout could be caught with marvelous rapidity. And so the days went by, camping, hunting, fishing, explor-

ON THE GRAND, MIDDLE PARK.

J. COLLIER, PHOTO.

ing, until we felt that a home in this place would be a "consummation most devoutly to be wished."

Fishing is one of the chief pleasures of a trip to Middle Park. The old fisherman who has been here before, will take you to the mouth of Beaver Creek, or to Williams' Fork, the mouth of Fraser, or to Troublesome Creek, for the finny game, for the old fisherman knows a thing or two, and likes to go to fresh waters which have not been fished out. From the Blue, below the springs, to the points mentioned above, up stream, there are plenty of trout, from the seven-pounder to the very small ones. Stout hooks and lines and true rods are needed, and with a little dexterity the trout fisher, accustomed to eastern streams, will have better success than he ever imagined was allotted to those who attempt to hook this shy and gamy fish.

One of the pleasantest excursions in Middle Park is up the valley, twenty-seven miles from the hot springs, by a road smooth and agreeable of travel, to Grand Lake, the source of the main fork of Grand River. Tucked away in a deep cover of the main mountain range, this lake is, indeed, a romantic spot. Cliffs hang frowning over its waters, on three sides, and all about the tall pines come almost down to the white sand beach. The river leaves the lake through a narrow gap, by which, also, the road enters. Down through the translucent waters of the lake the eye can penetrate to great depth, and from the cavernous and over-hanging rocks the echoes resound to the human voice in a remarkable manner, dying away, after several repetitions, in the mountain fastnesses above. There is a water-fall at the eastern extremity of the lake, but its roaring is so deceptive that it cannot be located by sound alone. The lake is thronged with trout, which can be caught with little or no effort. Two days at Grand Lake will never be regretted.

There is game in abundance, both on the mountains and in the park. Deer, mountain sheep, elk, bear, and antelope abound, but to hunt them requires much time and considerable trouble. Those who love such sport, however, can gratify their tastes to their hearts' content. As for our little party, we spent our time as taste dictated, some fishing, others hunting, while a few curiosity-seekers reaped rich harvests from the patches of agates which here abound. Amethyst, petrifactions, fossils, moss agates and kindred stones were gathered in abundance. But gathering specimens is an occupation one tires of, for these mountains are so rich in such articles that they accumulate rapidly and soon become a burden.

Time passes too rapidly when one is in the midst of such pleasures as we experienced here. There are scores of places one might go to, but they can best be determined upon as the fancy may dictate. Mountain life is one of freedom, and should not be hampered by any rules. The days are marvels of sunshine, the air as freshening as wine; for weeks the skies know no clouds. Cool nights succeed to warm days, and vigor comes of sleep. Beautiful flowers cover the landscape, and rich perfume is wafted on the breeze. The soughing pines on the mountain sides make music on the ear; the twinkling aspens and the dense foliage through the ravines make more grand the bleak and barren rocks above. As the days pass, we only regret that this season of mountain sojourning cannot be prolonged; but this country is so replete with attractive localities that we do not feel like losing one for the pleasure of tarrying in another.

This park is already becoming populated and utilized. The luxuriant grasses make it a desirable place for the grazing of cattle, and there are many herds here already. The means of access are now so good that the coming in and going out, during the summer months, present the slightest obstacles. We shall look to see it soon filled with herders, and pastoral pursuits followed by scores of ambitious men. More than four thousand tourists visited Middle Park last season.

There are routes into the park other than the one of which I have spoken. One from South Boulder has been used for years, but it is so tedious and difficult that it is not much traversed now. The tourist on this road rises to a point more than twelve thousand feet above the sea level, and travels for a long distance along the summit of the range, where a snow-storm in July or August is no novelty. There is plenty of romantic interest attaching to the routes, and the scenery is of that grand nature that passes description. Berthoud Pass, however, is very popular, and has long been in favor as a route for a railway over the mountains to the Pacific. It is about twenty miles from the Boulder Pass. The James' Peak trail, reached from Central City, is a splendid route, over which a buggy may be driven to the summit of the range. It forms a junction with the two other roads, in the valley of the Fraser, just after entering the park. It matters little how the tourist gets into the park, the scenery by either is varied and unparalleled.

SOUTH PARK AND TWIN LAKES.

CHAPTER IX.

SOUTH PARK AND TWIN LAKES.

THE easiest reached, and,— in the estimation of the most observant tourists who have preceded us in these delightful regions,— as well, the most attractive of the mountain parks, is South Park, as it is called, embracing within its area a more extensive grouping of peaks which rise to a greater height than do those of any other section here. It is dotted, also, with prosperous mining towns, and presents a succession of summer resorts incomparable for grand scenery and opportunities for sports. With a camping outfit and a pleasant party, the sojourn, whether it be long or short, is one which the tourist remembers only with pleasure. To climb lofty peaks and explore deep valleys, to revel in wild scenes and travel the by-ways of this Alpine country, is the ambition of those who come to pass the summer months in this American Switzerland. Having tarried awhile at other points, we at last turn our faces towards the South Park, and, for twenty days at least enjoy a season of mountaineering that knows no rival in this western land.

Of course there are various ways of going, either by carriages or wagons, or horseback, or by the stage. The latter is the most expeditious, and attended with little care, but is the least satisfactory. We chose the wagons, and, packing our tents and utensils, started, in the cool of an early morning, across the undulating plains which reach from Denver fifteen miles to the foot-hills. Then we passed through miles of valley studded with immense sand-stone rocks, until at last the road swung into Turkey Creek Cañon, and ran along a shelf cut upon the mountain side. Below dashed Turkey Creek, a beautiful stream, and above us hung beetling crags, while up and down the rugged gorge grew quaint pines and thick underbrush. As we ascend we meet with grassy meadows here and there, fringed by wooded slopes. Forty-four miles from Denver is the north fork of the Platte River. It is a large stream, filled with trout, the valley bordered by lofty mountains, and dotted with thrifty little farms. Twelve miles more and we come to the highest elevation before the park is reached, where the plateau is diversified with groves and grassy parks. Near the road is a little lake which water-fowls much frequent and near which deer and elk may be hunted. There is a road, at the right hand and just beyond this point, where one of the grandest views in Colorado may be obtained. Emerging from the zone of forest through which we have been passing, we come suddenly upon the rim of the park, and view the far-stretching country from an altitude of several hundred feet.

There is nothing to obstruct the vision. Miles away, on either hand, the giant mountains enclose the great area of level country which forms the park. The main range is on the right, snow-clad and superlatively grand; to the west, the serrated peaks of Saguache, dim and hazy; in the south, the Sangre de Cristo, which swings up into the east with glistening fields of snow. It was on one of those days, so rare to the rest of the world, when we stood viewing this scene,— a day when the atmosphere is intensely clear, and distant objects brought so near,— that we beheld, away off in the southwest, that natural symbol of the Christian faith which has given the mountain on which it lies the name of the Mount of the Holy Cross. It is formed by a pile of snow lying in the chasms, and presents to the view the perfect form of a gigantic cross.

Although the park may look flat from the point of observation of which I have just spoken, we find, upon descending, that it is seamed with valleys and covered with lofty wooded ridges. Across an arm of the park we pass twelve miles to Hamilton, and thence over the main range to Breckenridge, which little place is on the head waters of the Blue river, a stream that flows towards the Pacific. Those who enjoy trout fishing can here pursue this sport to the top of their bent. We return to Hamilton, and make the trip to Fairplay, the chief town in this region, and a base for touring observation in the park.

The grandest and most enduring monument man ever had is here — Mt. Lincoln, named in honor of the lamented president. The route from Fairplay to this mountain,— for we cannot pass it without an ascent to its summit,— is up a wagon road to Dudley, a mining camp, seven miles. From this point, we pass along a new and very steep wagon road, up the face of the mountain, to the Moose mine, on the north side of Mt. Bross. This is near the summit of the latter mountain, and here we follow a pack trail, for one and a half miles farther, to the Montezuma mine, and soon after come to the summit of Mt. Lincoln, which is only a few hundred feet beyond. Here we stand upon the rocky pinnacle, nearly three miles above the sea level. Below us, like an angry sea, float the clouds far down the mountain side, driven hither and thither by the shifting winds. Pike's Peak, away across the park to the east, and Buffalo Mountain, Silver Heels, and other giant peaks, stand up and above the cloudy sea like islands, and about their sides the mists come and fall like breakers on a rocky sea-girt shore. Strong winds soon blow away the clouds, and we get a view of the country below us. Two hundred peaks can be counted from Mt. Lincoln, all over 13,000 feet high, and three distinct ranges noted. The Front range, east, contains Mt. Torrey, Gray's Peak, Pike's Peak, Mt. Rosa, Mt. Evans, and others, from 14,000 to 14,200 feet in altitude. West of the Front range lie the great parks — North, Middle, South, and San Luis,— and parallel, and forty miles west, is what is known as the Park range. The highest points are near the junction of the Cross range that divides South Park from Middle Park. In the Mt. Lincoln group there are twenty peaks exceeding 13,000 feet in height. Twenty miles north is the Blue River group, with peaks from 13,000 to 13,200 feet high. West of the southern part of South Park is the National group, in which is Grand Mountain, 14,200 feet high; and there are ten others in this group above 14,000 feet. This range forms the grandest grouping of mountain heights on the continent.

Silver mining is followed in the vicinity of Fairplay. The district extends for six miles along the mountains, and is about two miles wide, and from 3,000 to 4,000 feet above the valley. The whole mountain mass was formerly called Mt. Lincoln, but, since the discovery of silver, it has been divided into districts. At the south end is Buckskin Mountain, next Mt. Bross, then Mt. Cameron, and at the north end, Mt. Lincoln. A slight depression, only, separates each.

The mountain road is high that leads us from Fairplay to Twin Lakes, but the country is covered with beautiful flowers whose colors are as brilliant as Tyrian dyes, and the air laden with their perfume. We pass the source of the Platte River, drop into the famous mining camps of California, Colorado and Frying Pan gulches, partake of water from noted mineral springs, and finally reach Twin lakes, nestled at the foot of the Saguache range, perfectly mountain locked. Trout are taken from these waters in great abundance. Life at these lakes is a perpetual round of enjoyment. Game of all descriptions is plentiful. The lower lake is three and a half miles long and two and a half miles wide; the upper lake about one-third as large. The mountain views here are remarkable. Near at hand, or adjacent, are Lake Mountain, Twin Peaks, La Plata Mountain, Mt. Elbert, and others, all noted for their extreme height, rugged contour, and some of them for their evident glacial erosions.

It was with regret that the days had passed so quickly that we left Twin Lakes, and went down the mountains, into the Arkansas Valley, past Chalk Creek, with its hot springs, near Mts. Howard and Yale. Up Trout Creek Cañon the road we had chosen carried us, and down again into South Park, past the Salt Works, in a northeasterly direction, towards Pike's Peak. The road was smooth and easily traveled. We visited the wonderful petrified stumps, near Castello's, camped in Florissant Park, just back of Pike's Peak, and gathered some splendid specimens from these petrified and agatized forest monarchs which flourished in the remote ages. The road begins a long ascent along the dividing ridge, in the forest on the summit of which we gained another panoramic view of the park behind us, the flanking mountain ranges, the Spanish Peaks to the southeast, and the ponderous base of Pike's Peak to the east. A few miles more, and we begin the descent through Ute Pass, winding around the great mountains and following the beautiful water-course towards the opening upon the plains at the base of the foot-hills. This route is one of weird interest and ever-changing scenery. As we descend, the passage between the mountain closes down upon us and becomes but a narrow gorge, devious in its windings, and walled in by immense and almost perpendicular rocks. We pass Ute Falls, and, a mile below, come suddenly into the open country that looks out upon the plains. The road takes us across the creek, and we are soon rolling past the soda springs at Manitou.

Here, amongst the cool cañons, we can pitch our movable habitation, and make a pleasant stay, visiting in the meantime the adjacent resorts — Garden of the Gods, Glen Eyrie, and Cheyenne Cañon, as well as making the ascent of Pike's Peak.

It may be well to remark that the journey from Twin Lakes may also be made from South Park to Cañon City, and thence around the base of Pike's Peak, north, through a hilly and rolling country, skirting the edges of the mountain timber region, and overlooking the wide-spreading plains, to Colorado City, and from that point either to Manitou or Colorado Springs, each only a couple of miles distant. The latter is the railway station for the Denver and Rio Grande Railway, by which Denver is reached.

COLORADO SPRINGS AND GARDEN OF THE GODS.

CHAPTER X.

COLORADO SPRINGS AND GARDEN OF THE GODS.

FROM Denver radiate five lines of railway, affording rapid and easy means of travel to the north, south and west, as well as joining the territory with the great east. Southward from Denver, and crawling slowly but surely to the land of Montezuma, is the Denver and Rio Grande Railway, a narrow-gauge thoroughfare, and the experimental test of the ensmalled iron road that is to revolutionize the railway system of the country. With rails three feet apart, cars that carry thirty-two to forty passengers, instead of sixty-four, as do the larger ones, and small engines, this has gained the appellation of the "baby railroad." It is, however, a very healthy and muscular infant. From Denver to Colorado Springs is seventy-six miles, to Pueblo one hundred and twenty miles, and to Cañon City one hundred and sixty miles. For the greater portion of the distance the road lies along a pleasant country, up the Platte River and Plum Creek, across the Divide — the watershed of the Arkansas and Platte rivers, north and south;

down Monument Creek and past Monument Park, a wonderful grove of spiral conglomerate rocks which the erosions of time have worn into fantastic shapes. The grade is very heavy to the summit of the Divide, nearly three thousand feet above Denver, and eight thousand feet above the sea. On the southern slope the descent is rapid, and the country changes from rugged hills, covered with dense pine forests, to a level and interesting expanse of prairie sloping from the east towards the foot-hills. Taken as a whole, this trip from Denver south affords much that is picturesque and satisfying to tourists, the curiosity-seeker, or the invalid.

It took us three days — days of unmixed pleasure — to make our journeys about the springs, and during that time we rambled through the Garden of the Gods, sauntered here and there, up to the falls in Ute Pass, climbed the rocks about the foot-hills, wandered over to Cheyenne Cañon, and basked in the genial sunshine of seemingly Italian weather. The Garden of the Gods has been much written about since the tide of scribblers set in this way, and the famed cañon above spoken of has also achieved deserved notoriety from their enthusiastic descriptions. The first is so named for its grotesque and gigantic rocks thrown into fantastic shapes by the convulsions of nature and worn by the elements during countless ages; the second spot is characterized by a grandeur of scenery, compressed into a narrow defile, surpassing nearly every other like section in this mountain range. Being of that slow

and easy class of tourists who believe in enjoying whatever nature has made and man has brought within the route of travel, we took our time and looked upon these interesting things with the eyes of careful study. Many of the fast travelers of the day can "do" these points in a few hours. They are the ones who go through the land at lightning speed, with a dinner perpetually a few hours ahead, and with more thought of their appetite than the storing of useful information. This is the way a great many people go through these gardens, partake of these waters, and view this cañon. Or, if they can get a glimpse of the red sandstone piles from the hotel steps, and drink a bottle of the water brought over to the railway station, and have an experienced citizen point out the locality where the cañon is, they are satisfied, and, feeling that they have done their duty and spent their money religiously, they turn their faces homeward fully satisfied that they have seen through the vision of others and heard from others' lips the details of the famous Rocky Mountain region.

Those who have any desire to see for themselves, and who are not satisfied with simple hearsay, will take ample time to investigate the points of which I speak in these pages. It is but a short distance from the hotel to the point where the road turns into the Garden of the Gods; but the trip may weary one unless he makes it in some vehicle. On every hand are masses of sandstone, white and red, some rising to a great height, and all dipping more or less to the west. They are scattered in picturesque confusion. The chief point of attraction is the Beautiful Gate, that opens into the Gardens proper, and through which is seen one of the most magnificent sights man ever beheld. The opening is perhaps fifty feet in width; on either side stand huge piles of sandstone, rising over three hundred feet; in the centre of the gateway a pillar thirty feet in height, and away beyond, miles away, stately Pike's Peak, with here and there a bank of snow upon its cold gray sides. Of course a preëmptor's cabin near at hand mars this splendid scene, and on the rocks are glaring black letters announcing that John Smith's stereoscopic views are the best in the world, and that some new-fangled soothing syrup will put babies to sleep quicker and make them sleep longer than any other nostrum in existence. These little things fall upon one's rhapsodies like a wet blanket; but they testify to the universal Yankee's presence and business instincts. We can but believe that this omnipresent genius would have advertised the newest patent bitters on the Saviour's cross, and ornamented His tomb with some Israelite's secondhand clothing advertisement, had he been so fortunate as to have existed then. The Yankee's mark is on every trail that civilization has opened.

This Garden consists of a tract of land of a little less than five hundred acres in extent, hemmed in by mountains on the west and north, bordered by ravines on the south, and old red sandstone rocks on the east, which

GARDEN OF THE GODS

J. COLLIER, PHOTO.

shut it entirely out from the plains. Vegetation is slight, the landscape being dotted here and there only with piñon and pine trees, and the grasses scarce, except in the low valleys near water-courses.

The tradition of these rocks is interesting. It is that this was once the abode of Jupiter — he who from high Olympus flung the bolts of his wrath down upon the world; that, before his exploits and conquests in the Grecian archipelago, he lived and ruled in this beautiful garden; that here the forces of the gods met in battle strong, and, hurling these rocks at each other, caused them to assume their novel shapes! Those familiar with the locality will take you to Jupiter's cave, and also to the great hollow in the rocks where, the story goes, the beautiful Venus was wont to perform her matutinal ablutions!

The lover of the beautiful and novel in nature can here spend hours in contemplation of these interesting objects, with new attractions constantly coming into view, and objects of scientific interest rising to the observation. Imaginative tourists can fashion whatever the mind dictates from these quaint stones — stately castles with frowning battlements, fragmentary cathedral windows, gigantic figures suggesting various animals, and hundreds of other equally fanciful objects. There is scarcely a limit to the changing scenes, caused by every turn amongst the curious rocks.

MANITOU SPRINGS AND PIKE'S PEAK.

CHAPTER XI.

MANITOU SPRINGS AND PIKE'S PEAK.

AM inclined to believe that the people who named Colorado Springs did it with the willful intent to deceive the public, for there never was a spring there, and never will be. Like a great many other places in Colorado, it is named after something it never had, and is, therefore, a misnomer. It is five miles from the Springs to the springs — that is, the railway station is five miles from Manitou, where these soda and iron springs bubble from the ground. No wonder that people are confused and do not know whether they are at the springs when they are at Manitou, or whether they are at Colorado Springs when they are at the springs.

They call this place the Saratoga of Colorado, because there are waters here that carry soda and mineral properties, and because Manitou is frequented during the summer season by the *élite* of the territory, eastern *parvenus*, substantial tourists and ailing invalids. It is a desirable sojourning place for one with weak lungs and debilitated constitution, for the air builds up the one and the water regulates the other. There are splendid walks and cosy retreats, and if the lady is only interestingly invalided she can pass the time pleasantly drinking water and waltzing in the pavilion.

As the summer draws on, the butterflies of fashion wing their way down here and develop their gorgeous social colors for the attraction of the masculine eye. For medicinal springs have their votaries at fashion's shrine, in nearly as large numbers as they have mendicants who seek healing at the waters' side. Life at the springs is divided between flirtations, water-drinking, excursions and mountain climbing. And of these interesting occupations there is enough for all who come.

The reputation of the springs at Manitou has spread to a national renown, and the waters are sought by people from far and near, for the healing of various ailments. They extend along the beautiful creek which runs through this valley — the Fontaine-qui-Bouille — and are of various character, soda and iron. Some of them bubble out upon the banks of the creek and discharge their healing waters into the stream, while others are at the very edge of the creek. Since the spot has become a resort, the springs have been walled up and made very attractive. Rustic bridges have been thrown across the Fontaine, and delightful walks laid out. In the early morn it is no uncommon thing to meet scores of people standing about the chief soda spring,— the Manitou, which has been covered with a tasty rustic house,— waiting for a draught of the sparkling water.

RAINBOW FALLS, MANITOU.

J. COLLIER, PHOTO.

These springs are all named in Indian nomenclature, each name conveying an idea of the characteristics of the water.

Far up in one of the glens is the largest iron spring, the water of which is very beneficial in its effects upon the system. Those who cannot stand the fatigue of clambering the roadway that leads up to it, can find this water in the valley below, brought down for drinking purposes. In short, this locality appears to be a sanitarium where the afflicted may come and bathe in or drink of the healing waters. Tourist and invalid alike will find both pleasure and physical relief here.

It is but a short distance, comparatively, from here to the summit of Pike's Peak, which mountain stands but a few miles away. An excellent trail has been made, so that the fatigues of mountain climbing are to a great measure done away with, and it is an easy matter to now ride on horseback to the very summit. A great advantage, this, over the days when it was almost an impossibility to scale the rocks, and was a journey fraught with untold dangers.

Pike's Peak stands like a sentinel on the outposts of the mountain chain, being at the edge that flanks the great plains. Its summit is flat and covered with immense rocks, about eighty-four acres in extent. To arrive at the summit before the day dawns, and to watch the coming of the light that floods the far-off eastern plains, and casts its dark shadows across the lower hills, is an experience long remembered. As the darkness below gives way to the glorious sunlight, and the streams glisten like silver ribbons across the emerald plains, the landscape unfolds its marvelous beauty gradually. The mountain tops have long before stepped forth from darkness and taken their place one by one in the grand review. "Jocund day stands tip-toe on the misty mountain tops;" peak after peak seems answering to the roll-call of the great Creator. Down upon the plains morning dawns long after the crests have felt the genial glow. Far off into the South Park, west; south towards New Mexico; east across the great plains, stretched out like a floor; north beyond that other grim warder, Long's Peak; all these the eye takes in with an extent of country that can scarcely be comprehended at one glance. Here the approaching storms are signaled to the country from an observatory, the employees of which live here winter and summer. In the winter season it is far from being a desirable abode; but in their strong and warm house they experience but little of the inclemency of the borean blasts and driving snow.

Within easy walking distance from the hotel at Manitou is the Ute Pass, through which travel to the South Park passes from this vicinity. It is a romantic spot, and, winding amongst the rocks, presents a multitude of attractions. Only a short distance up are the Ute Falls, where a splendid descent is made, in an unbroken sheet, fifty or sixty feet. The roadway runs close to the edge of the precipice, below which flows the creek. On the other hand, the rocks tower above to an immense height. At places the pass opens wide, and is filled with rank vegetation. The trees form arches above the roadway, here and there, and little houses, tucked away in the aspens and pines, now and then suddenly appear, and give evidence of life in the midst of the entrancing objects with which nature has here been so lavish.

Time spent at Manitou is well spent. Idaho Springs, and this point of which I here write, are the two favorite and most accessible resorts, both for those who have no ailments and are traveling for pleasure, and those who seek relief in the tonic of the air, rambles amongst the hills, and guzzling of the waters.

A TRIP TO GLEN EYRIE.

CHAPTER XII.

A TRIP TO GLEN EYRIE.

AS the visitor to Colorado Springs stands on the hotel veranda in the early morning, awaiting the carriage in which he is to make the trip to that entrancing spot, Glen Eyrie, his vision will naturally sweep across the low lands to the west, and up the rugged mountains, until at last it rests upon the summit of that Titan pile of granite, Pike's Peak. There, lights and shades, sunlight and shadow, and the borean blasts, strive for mastery, and, above and beyond, the fleecy clouds seem bending to kiss away the snows. The changeful beauties of this scene are never tiresome, and the longer they are dwelt upon the more fascinating do they become. As we scan the country to the left, Cheyenne Mountains rise before the view, while beyond and higher up rise innumerable peaks nameless since creation's dawn. Far to the right, and sweeping around Pike's Peak, is a depression in the mountain range that mars somewhat the artistic groupings of the foot-hills about Ute Pass; farther still, but lower down, is the Garden of the Gods,—distinguishable by the red sandstone piles,— and, just beyond the latter, in a mountain defile, Glen Eyrie, the wild and weird home of a romantic railway president.

It has been very truly said that the Coloradan of to-day has no cause to envy the easterners their Saratoga, as he paces up and down this hotel piazza and mingles his full-flavored Havana with the lovely air, quite unbreathed before, which floats down upon him from the snow-peaks of the range. And the tourist has cause to feel that he has been privileged to enjoy the unspeakable beauties of nature from a civilized and humanized standpoint.

It will not do to indulge too much in rhapsodical reveries. The roadway from Colorado Springs to Glen Eyrie lies along the western slope of the "hog-back," a low, level hill, and then passes over its summit. It is called the cut-off, by reason of being the shorter route. There is a point on the summit of this hill called Kalarama, from the beautiful view it affords, and here the tourist may obtain a foretaste of the scene beyond. Below us, here, winds a sparkling stream,— ribbon-like, so far is it down,— and fringed with cottonwood and alders, far to the south. This valley is as delightful a one as man ever looked upon for picturesque simplicity. There are massive mountains to the west of us, while between them and the elevation upon which we stand are the high piles of red and white sandstone which rise so strangely and form such grotesque figures in the Garden of the Gods. Our journey takes us to the right, down a steep roadway, across the brook, through the thick *chaparral* of bushes and vines which form an archway here and there, over a rustic bridge, and suddenly upon a rustic cottage, the porter's lodge to this vast estate, inside. Around an abrupt projection of rock we pass, which resolves itself into an impregnable wall as we ride along. We turn and view this natural fortress. Three hundred feet above us, in a crevice of the rock, may be seen the deserted eyries of the eagles, from which this spot is named. A mile away from us, perhaps, there stands a mass of red sandstone, called the Organ Rock, which seems only waiting for some genie of the mountains to come and touch its keys. Beyond this is a pile of white sandstone, carved by the winds and rains into so many shapes that it looks to the casual beholder like some feudal castle, transplanted by magic to this quiet recess of the Rocky Mountains.

The road we are traversing winds and twists amongst the shattered rocks that lie scattered about the ground, and every turn brings a fresh surprise and adds new beauties to the scene. Wherever we turn, we find confronting us sandstone rocks of fantastic shapes and pleasing colors, "from brightest vermilion, through orange and yellow, to almost dazzling white; planted by nature with pine, douglasii, spruce and cedar," all presenting, in its romantic beauty, a scene scarcely to be surpassed. We ride on and up the roadway until the crowning surprise of the journey meets our view — a beautiful house perched upon the rocks, and from which a commanding view of the whole valley, or glen, may be obtained.

None other than a Yankee would have utilized this locality for the purpose of residence. It is a fine summer retreat, away from the noise of the world, where naught breaks the quiet but the moaning pines above and around, and the musical murmuring of the water in Queen's Cañon beyond. In the winter season, with the driving storm, the snow-covered roads, the whistling winds, it must, indeed, be a dreary habitation. The house is elegantly furnished, and is decorated with many specimens of mountain animals, as well as battle trophies of its owner. Nature has done everything for this glen, but a perpetual residence here is not desirable.

We find many other points with great attractions, by going up Queen's Cañon, — an enticing opening into the mountains, — and visiting the Devil's Punch Bowl, and the succession of falls, each one of which might be taken for a naiad's bath. This is a typical mountain gorge; many are larger, but few more beautiful. The road that takes us out of the glen, on the north side of the brook, gives us new views fully as charming as were those on entering. We pass needles of sandstone standing nearly two hundred feet in air, and leaning like the tower of Pisa. Another glimpse is had of the eagle nests; we toss the porter a bit of change, rumble over the bridge, rattle under the arching bushes, and finally find that we have the choice of two roads to make our way home — the one by which we came, or another down the creek, and through Colorado City, to our hotel. We took the latter, and had a ride over a poor road, saw a town that used to boast the capital of the territory, but is somewhat dilapidated now, and took a delightful supper as the sun was setting, feeling happy over the thought that a day had been spent profitably.

TO CHEYENNE CANON.

CHAPTER XIII.

TO CHEYENNE CAÑON.

IT is a drive of several miles from Manitou to Cheyenne Cañon, across a fine section of farming country, from the edge of which, upon the bluffs, a good view of Colorado Springs and outlying sections, away to the Divide at the north,— the high country that breaks the water-courses of the Arkansas and the Platte rivers,— can be obtained. The roadway takes us to the mouth of the cañon, and, leaving our horses there, we make the remainder of the distance afoot. It is nearly three miles to the point we wish to reach, and the novice in mountaineering will find this distance apparently stretching into as many leagues before he has picked his weary way over the rocks and up to the falls beyond. The trail — such as there is, for it is not an easy place in which to make a pathway — leads through tangled underbrush, on each side of the little stream which dashes and foams and makes music between the granite walls. The pathway crosses and recrosses the brook so many times that one becomes tired of counting the fordings, up the rocks and down, and along the water's edge. Care is essential to a journey of this cañon, lest while enraptured with gazing upon the mountain sides and admiring the granite cleft, the foot slip and meditation receive the reward of careless travel in the cooling waters of the brook.

Passing into the cañon about a quarter of a mile, the rocks suddenly close in behind, and the first impressions are obtained of the grandeur yet to come. Another turn, and we clamber up on the side of the rocky incline that sweeps to the water's edge, and on our right, high above us, towards the ethereal blue, is St. Peter's dome, and directly in front Pulpit Rock, from which it would seem some giant expounder might proclaim salvation to the world. At this point begins the most attractive portion of the cañon, which is but the separation of a giant mountain from its summit to its base. Again the walls become almost perpendicular, the level summits, on either side, apparently not a stone's throw apart, twenty-two hundred feet above the level of the creek. We go on and on, up the trail, across the shallow stream, and the defile still maintains its mammoth proportions. The rocks close in behind, as the stream turns here and there, and the oppressiveness of the grandeur and massiveness of the scene beggars description. Two miles and a half of the climbing,—but it does one good and makes the muscles strong,—and the roar of the cataract suddenly burst upon our ears. The roaring grew louder and louder as we stumbled on, panting for breath, when suddenly we emerged into a chamber, over a ledge on one side of which a seething and sparkling sheet of water tumbles full thirty feet or more. The air was damp and the rocks spray-covered, and into the dark nook a shaft of sunlight fell from a rent in the mountains above.

There were evidences of the presence of humanity in this far-away and solitary cañon, at some time not long preceding our advent. On a pile of rocks, just below the falls, and made of drift-wood, was a rude cross. The universal Yankee had been there too, and left his mark indelibly carved on the base of that cross. There were his initials, but he must have been a Yankee of elegant leisure and out of business, else he would have daubed some "ready relief" advertisement high up on the granite walls, and written a verse commemorative of his jaunt up the cañon. As he had set the example, and as we are Yankees, too, we added our letters to the others and felt serenely happy when the deed was done.

This cross, symbol of faith, was raised by a woman, the first of her sex to penetrate to this cascade. She was ambitious to make her mark, and she manifested more energy and perseverance, and showed more muscle than do the average of the female kind. Now, however, since the way has been cleared, and the trail is open, ladies can go up with the utmost ease, provided they are not afraid of water, slippery rocks and the prospect of fatigue.

There is a trail up the mountain side, just below the fall, by means of which we can ascend to the bench above the cataract, and, climbing farther up, we have opened to the view a succession of falls, six in all, rising one above the other at almost regular intervals, the remotest and highest several miles removed from the point of our observation. Right and left the mountains tower high above the stream; below, we look down into the cañon for some distance over the route we have traversed; and above, the bright blue sky spans the opening in the hills, unflecked by even a tiny cloud. We see the eagles circling here and there about the mountain peaks.

But one cannot dwell in these regions long, for there are other sights to see. Already the journey had consumed several hours, and we turned reluctantly to retrace our steps. The way down hill is quickly traversed, compared with the ascent. Up and down the hill-sides, and over the jagged rocks, down the slides of disintegrated granite, and into the water perhaps, cautiously stepping over boulders and swinging across the streams, dodging flying limbs and stooping to escape the thick underbrush, until the plains open to view, we come down to the level, pass out into the broad sunlight, enter our carriages and go back to the hotel and a good supper, happy to know that the day has been profitably spent, and that the appetite has developed in direct ratio with the exertion of mountain climbing.

SOUTHERN COLORADO.

CHAPTER XIV.

SOUTHERN COLORADO.

SOUTHERN Colorado opens a new field to the tourist, and presents a different phase of life from that with which we meet in the northern districts. The country assumes more of the characteristics of a warmer climate, and here are found, amongst the large American population, the forerunners of the peculiar civilization of New Mexico and the more remote sections.

Pueblo is the principal city of the southern portion of this great territory. It is situated on the banks of the Arkansas River, which stream makes its exit from the mountains about forty miles above this point. In the matter of beauty, Pueblo has no distinguishing features to make it particularly noteworthy. It is built upon a broad level basin, the soil rather sandy and somewhat impregnated with alkali. The streets are regularly laid out, in the main, but the buildings — with some few exceptions — are small and unpretentious. In the matter of business, the city occupies a leading position, as its feeders reach south to New Mexico, west into the mountains, and, in fact, in all directions over a vast extent of country. Like many other cities in this western land, it is ambitious to acquire all the rail connections it possibly can, and to this end has labored unceasingly. Somewhat of a rival of Denver,— although I can hardly see how the success of the one is to materially affect the prosperity of the other,— Pueblo is continually exerting herself to monopolize the southern trade. The visitor to this city cannot fail to notice this. During our stay in this city,— which was of necessity brief, as we were anxious to visit all the other points of interest we possibly could in the time allotted us,— we saw that we were amongst an energetic people, full of local pride, and anxious to establish a leading commercial centre in this portion of Colorado. We found that Pueblo is flanked by rich agricultural and grazing lands, and that these industries are developing under the direction of the rapidly-increasing stockmen and ranchmen, who have been led here by the superior inducements of climate, grasses, and fertility of soil. We found the city prosperous in its growth, and hopeful of unbounded success in the matter of its material advancement.

Las Animas and Trinidad are other cities of southern Colorado,— reached by stage from Pueblo,— which have, within a few years past, risen to a position of importance. The former may be reached by rail, from Kit Carson, while the latter is on the old Santa Fé stage road. Las Animas is in the heart of the finest grazing country in Colorado, and is noted as being a shipping point for cattle. The town has grown rapidly, and bids fair to become second to no other point in the Western cattle market. Trinidad has, of late, under the impetus afforded by the increasing white population, grown rapidly. Developments of coal and other minerals have added greatly to the industries of the place, and, with the rail connection the city hopes soon to have, the growth of Trinidad is an assured fact.

Forty miles from Pueblo, by the narrow-gauge railroad, and at the base of the mountains, is Cañon City, where is located the territorial penitentiary. This town, with its many surroundings, is becoming an important summer point. Nature has been lavish of her gifts here; there are iron beds, coal deposits, oil wells, mineral springs, and mines of precious metals, contiguous, which will prove of great value, and which are being rapidly developed by capitalists and prospectors. The mineral springs, which are quite near to the city, are prized highly for their medicinal qualities, and are becoming more fully appreciated every day.

But a short distance above Cañon City, the Arkansas river makes its exit from the mountains, the gorge through which it runs, known as the Arkansas Cañon, being one of the most remarkable for wild scenery in this section. For miles the water-course makes its way between the perpendicular granite walls, which open only wide enough to form the bed of the stream. The cañon twists and turns its way through the adamantine hills, the river, thousands of feet below all points of observation, looking like a tiny stream surging its way over the boulders at the bottom, and dashing itself into spray against the impeding walls. The scene here is wild, weird, and romantic; it is superlatively grand, and incomparably awful. Several adventurous persons have attempted to shoot the cañon in boats and on rafts, but have met with disaster before the journey was half accomplished. Tourists who visit the southern portion of this territory should not fail to visit the Arkansas Cañon.

We found in this vicinity inviting resorts for quiet summering and pleasurable mountaineering. The days were refreshing, the mountain roads agreeable, and we returned north delighted with the experiences gained by the brief sojourn in the country "beyond the Divide," as it is termed by the Denver people.

A WEEK AMONG THE UTES.

GARDEN OF THE GODS

J. COLLIER, PHOTO.

CHAPTER XV.

A WEEK AMONG THE UTES.

ON our trip into Southern Colorado we departed somewhat from the regular route of tourist travel, and made a journey to the Ute Indian Reservation, which lies over the Cochetopa Pass, and is adjacent to the now noted San Juan mining country. The Ute nation, which numbers about five thousand souls, formerly had a very large "farm" in the western portion of the Territory, embracing an area of over nineteen million acres. Of this, about four million acres, in which is situate the San Juan district, has been ceded back to the Government. This still leaves them a very handsome domain on which to hunt and lead their nomadic life.

We made the excursion from Pueblo, all the distance in carriages, nearly three hundred miles, *via* the Sangre de Cristo Pass, Fort Garland, the Rio Grande River, Saguache, and the Cochetopa Pass. From Pueblo to Badito — the foot of the first pass — is a stretch of sage-brush and plains, prairie-dogs and piñon-trees, the Greenhorn and the Huerfano Rivers, with a good dinner at Miller's, and a restless night at Badito. The Sangre de Cristo is an easy drive the greater portion of the way, but some of it is so stony and steep that none other than a Mexican bull-whacker or an innocent and uninformed traveler would ever think of crossing it. The redeeming features of the pass are the scenery of the western slope and the trout-fishing.

We crossed the San Luis Valley, and camped two nights on the north bank of the Rio Grande River, there a handsome stream, and filled with monster trout. We camped in the Saguache Valley, also near the summit of the Cochetopa Pass, and on the sixth day from Pueblo reached the Los Pinos Agency, where, we had been told, the Utes, to the number of three thousand, had assembled. We were now on the Pacific Slope, the waters here running towards the Gulf of California.

These Indians are queer specimens of humanity. They gather about you with childish simplicity, admire your blankets with envy, and beg systematically for sugar; they ride fearlessly, shoot skillfully, dress outrageously, live dirtily, and negotiate with visitors most diplomatically. They are the wards of the nation, and yet the nation treats them with the utmost consideration; they are the Ishmaelites of the plains and mountains, and yet they are received with open arms and lovingly caressed into filial obedience; they stand defiantly off and warn you from the possessions they have acquired by reversion, and then come down and beg for presents, and consider a refusal a cause for trouble. They are a strange admixture of human nature, untutored yet shrewd, and they are never so well understood as when met with in their villages and seen about their agencies. One acquires there an idea of the aborigines' laziness, indolence, cheek, and natural untidiness.

We were at the Agency some five or six days, circulating amongst the red constitutents of the Government who had flocked there to draw rations. A Ute village, I suppose, is much like any other Indian village — is just as dirty, the tepees are of the same shape, the women quite as frowzy, the bucks just as dignifiedly lazy, and the pappooses just as naked. It affords some pleasure — perhaps real satisfaction — to one accustomed to the precise and elegant fashions of the metropolitan centers, to witness with what abandon these people attire themselves. When we rode into the village, some of the high counselors and bucks of elevated position, youth and hoary age, came out to see us. And they were dressed in their good clothes, too. It was quite apparent that the Ute fashion designer, or the Ute tailors, generally, had set their wits and their fingers to work to prepare for the occasion. How childlike and bland did one old heathen, with a variegated countenance, appear, as he rode up attired in a dilapidated shirt; and how charming was the sweet-faced and modern Minnehaha, her hair hanging in unkempt looseness over her mouth, and whose lower extremities were attired in a charming pair of peg-top buckskin pantaloons fringed with the coarse hair of some old Arapahoe sinner! I shall not soon forget the picturesque scene presented by a youth of seven summers, who, attired in the *négligé* costume of a dirty hickory shirt, ripped on both sides, from the bottom to the arm-hole, went waltzing up the road, while a caressing breeze sent both sides fluttering towards the heavens. Then, too, there was a dignified cuss attired in an old-fashioned muzzle-loading rifle and a pair of red moccasins! There was another gentle savage, on a rearing and fractious *burro*, who came prancing around in a full-dress suit of whitewash, scolloped on the edges, and looped up with yellow ochre. There were others equally elegantly, if not so fashionably, attired. Ute styles are simple — being principally yellow and red paint and lamp-black, laid on in fantastic stripes. Fashions comprise a little of everything. If a Ute gets a pair of old army shoes, a shirt that has not known water for fifteen years, an army coat discarded on account of rags, infantry shoulder-straps, navy-stripes, a plug hat made by the hatter to Old Noah the ship-builder, and then slings a lot of beads promiscuously around his head and neck and body, he is rigged out in a costume warranted to command envy, if not respect, amongst the others of the tribe. A buck is a heavy swell on styles, if he doesn't save a cent.

The day we arrived there and became settled in our quarters, we were waited on by various delegations, young and old, all of whom stood around like a lot of statues, or a line of Prussian soldiers, and, for a long time, never spoke a word. They were evidently very much rejoiced to see us, and when we nodded familiarly to some superannuated old buffer, and affected a sort of patronizing air towards some of these superior beings, in the vain belief that we might be entertaining some angel of a chief unawares, we were generally rewarded with a stupid grin or a mumbled piece of Ute and Spanish. Frequently some familiar piece of human dirt would walk into the tent and sit complacently down on the bed, and regale us with an amiable and interesting conversation in choice Ute and abominable English — in which one hopelessly endeavored to master the other.

A person who goes for the first time amongst these human vermin whom the Peace Commission are ticketing through by lightning express to the high estate of civilization,— without a stopping place on the road,— is a little amused and very much surprised and horrified at the manner in which the Indians live.

There was a grand display of military prowess on the part of the Utes. They are very much like white people in this respect; they delight in showing how strong they are and how easily they could vanquish their foes — providing, of course, the foes were not too many for them. They arrayed themselves in all their feathers and paint and fuss, and dress and undress uniforms, and came down in the most gorgeous array and unbroken line of battle, amid the discharge of fire-arms, the beating of tom-toms, and a discordant nasal melody for which they are noted. They were mounted on horses, and numbered about three hundred warriors, the women and children following in the rear. The men were all attired in their war costumes, and many of them were hideous and repulsive to the sight. Several, quite naked, and painted in the most horribly grotesque manner, were disgusting objects. Others were quite gay, assuming as well considerable dignity of station, and displaying a vast amount of pride over their unapproachable and immaculate attire. It was their pleasure to show us their mode of procedure whenever an enemy's scalp falls into their hands, by giving a scalp dance. It consisted of dancing and shouting, screaming, drumming and yelling, while an old, haggard and wrinkled squaw kept the men to their work by joining in the breakdown and working assiduously in the semi-religious observance. This was to us a weird, strange sight, and the dirt and the vermin, and the stolid indifference of the participants disappeared entirely from the mind, and in their place, as we watched this rite, came up unpleasant imaginings of very lively "shinning" around, should that pack of ferocious, and yet very tame, hyenas, turn loose upon us. They used up all the breath and powder and muscle they had, passed in review again, and then went off singing, and after this all was quiet for the time.

An Indian died in the village one night, and there was inconsolable mourning on the part of his family for a couple of days. An old squaw — the widow probably — struck the key-note of her grief nearly at high C, about daybreak, and covered the whole musical scale with her lamentations before the day was done. She had her hair cut off, and then persuaded some twenty other squaws to help her out in the matter of howling. After this she attested her love for the dear departed by having his horses and dogs shot. At the same time there was an Indian sick in one of the lodges, and the medicine man made a great ado over his maladies. They use about the same "medicine" for both — howl when they're dead, howl when they are sick; and when everybody is well and they haven't anything in particular to mourn over, they sit around and howl for joy.

Human nature is human nature — whether in an Indian or a white person; but, unlike that "quality of mercy" we read of, this is strained. I saw a sight in the Indian village, one afternoon, that showed how nearly akin the red and white women are, and how the instincts of humanity do not differ. A little girl of three or four years had a papoose board in her arms, and on the board an Indian doll, covered with wicker work and a small piece of red cloth. She cared for it as carefully as a white child does for her imaginary offspring, and probably felt the same instinctive yearning for maternity.

This Indian nation lives in the mountains of Colorado, although there are one or two detached tribes who make their homes in New Mexico, refusing to remain upon the reservation set apart for them. They earn a precarious living, which they feel is due them at the expense of the whites, by begging government annuities, stealing, and shooting game, frequently spending weeks down on the plains hunting the bison. It is their custom to make frequent visits to the settlements, but they have never, of late, shown any disposition to inaugurate a warfare on the white people. Various bands go up to Denver, frequently, to see the governor and get some annuities, and are there subjects of interest to the strangers and of disgust on the part of the old citizens. The Ute nation is ruled by a chief who is as diplomatic and honorable as an Indian can well be. He is also inclined to ape the customs of his white friends. When I last saw this dignified fellow at the agency, he was making ready to start away, on a tour of inspection, perhaps, in an old-fashioned barouche that he had purchased of some settler over in the Saguache Valley. He was provided with two American horses and an Indian coachman; and, sitting inside the vehicle, with a spy-glass over his left arm, and his squaw by his side, the equipage rolled across the plateau towards the mountain pass, the head chief displaying all the *sang-froid* and luxurious manner of a veritable aristocrat.

The route from the Indian Agency, by which we returned, lay through the north end of the San Luis Valley, past the hot springs into the Arkansas Valley, over Poncha Pass, through Trout Creek Cañon into South Park, and thence through Ute Pass to Manitou, near Colorado Springs. The scenery of this route is grand to the most eminent degree, and the road extends through a charming section of country the greater portion of the distance. Fish and game abound, and there is nothing lacking to make the trip one of pleasure and profit.

On the trip from Fort Garland to the Los Pinos Agency we were curious to visit the new towns of Loma and Del Norte, which have been developed by the San Juan mining excitement, and through which the route lies to this very rich country. The one thing uppermost in the minds of the people there was mines. We heard little but conversation on "rock" and "claims," "feet" and "discoveries," "leads," "silver," "Baker's Park," "the Animas," and other topics all interlarded with the, to us, most incomprehensible of miners' phrases. The streets were filled with enthusiastic prospectors, and with persistent and pestiferous blackmailers endeavoring to cheat honest miners out of their dues. The grocer, weighing sugar and tea, discoursed eloquently upon the last return from the Bully Boy, or the prospective development of the Sarah Jane; the barber, drawing the glittering steel across his customer's face, paused now and then to recount how he had "struck it rich" in Squeedunk Cañon, and how he expected to lay aside the razor in a few days when that sale was made that would carry him to the highest tide of financial prosperity; the hotel keeper abstractedly inquired, "how many shares?" as we put our names upon the register, thinking all the time of the new company in which he was a stockholder; the bar-keeper mixed Last Chance cocktails and Little Giant sours as he dealt out his villainous liquors. Everything was covered with gold and silver bearing quartz; the windows were filled with it; it stood in the street; we found it mixed with our food; everybody had tons of it; everybody was prospectively rich, everybody enthusiastic, everybody happy — except the "pilgrims" who had walked there and had not a dollar or a silver lode to call their own.

The San Juan country is developing very rapidly, is possessed of rich deposits of gold and silver, and will become one of the chief points in Colorado. Cities are building up along the road to the mines; the way is easy over the mountains, and thousands of people are going in to possess the land, which, of late, has been ceded back to the Government. There is also much excitement over the Elk River mines, beyond the Indian Agency.

AGRICULTURE, MINING, STOCK, AND CLIMATE.

CHAPTER XVI.

AGRICULTURE, MINING, STOCK, AND CLIMATE.

WHILE journeying over the territory of Colorado, the tourist has ample opportunity to study the material resources of the country, which show themselves on every hand. It is a land of great promise. The people who came in here during the excitement of 1859, when the news of gold discoveries went abroad, like wildfire through prairie grass, had little thought of laying the foundation of a future great State. They came, urged on by the desire to amass fortunes, which end achieved, they would be content to leave the mountains and the plains, with their untold privations and hardships, and go back to eastern homes to spend luxuriously what they had gained laboriously. But this was the good luck of very few of those pioneers. Others retraced their steps disconsolately. The adventurous remained, and, by their persistent operations and rightly-directed energies, began to develop what has since proved one of the richest, most substantial, and easiest accessible of the territories of the United States. In the early days it was thought impossible to till the soil here. The minds of people had become so filled with the idea that the plains were, and would always remain, a barren desert, that agriculture was, for the time, considered an uncertain and impractical pursuit. Experiments, however, proved the soil to be remarkably productive, in the bottoms of streams where the land was sub-irrigated; and then the ingenuity of man, following the examples of the people of other arid countries, began to plan rude irrigation ditches, which carried the water upon the high lands. To-day agriculture is followed by a great proportion of the citizens of the territory. The valleys are wonderfully fertile and productive, and yield cereals that are accounted superior to those of any section east or west. Colorado wheat has now a national reputation, and its flour is held to be superior to that of any of the older wheat-growing districts. To be cultivated, the soil of Colorado must be irrigated; but as the never-failing mountain streams furnish plenty of water for this purpose, the year round, and as irrigation ditches are more reliable than rain, crops are matured with certainty. Along the base of the foot-hills, far down the fertile valleys, toward the plains, the country is spotted with thrifty farms, which produce abundant crops. The Platte Valley is noted for its fertility, from the cañon where it bursts upon the plains, along its entire course through the territory; also, the Cache-a-la-Poudre, from Greeley to the mountains; Left Hand and St. Vrain creeks; Big Thompson and the Little Thompson creeks; Boulder Creek, Clear, Turkey and Bear creeks; Coal and Clear creeks — all tributary to the Platte River. The Monument, and the Fontaine-qui-Bouille; the Arkansas, Greenhorn, St. Charles and Huerfano rivers; these are all noted agricultural regions, fast populating with a hardy, industrious and intelligent class of people. In addition to these outlying agricultural regions, there are many sections, over the mountains, in the warm valleys, where farming is pursued with rich results and large profits.

The development of Colorado has established to a certainty the excellence of its natural grasses, with which the plains abound. As a result, it has come to be known as the paradise of stock men. Tempered by an equable climate; visited by comparatively light snows, below the Divide; having sparkling waters in the streams which make their way across the plains, from the mountains, it is one of the most desirable places in America for the raising of cattle for the eastern markets. Scores of Texas drovers drive their herds to this territory, recognizing the nutritious qualities of the grasses on the grazing ranges, and the safety of stock from the despoiling hand of marauding Indians. Sheep are raised in great numbers, and this industry has received impetus of late, attention being paid to the grading up of Mexican ewes by imported bucks. While cattle roam at pleasure through the winter season, sheep require more care. The raising of cattle, sheep and horses has already developed a leading resource of the territory, and Colorado beef and mutton and wool are becoming as noted as Colorado wheat and flour. Stock farms, too, are becoming numerous, where thorough-bred animals are fast multiplying.

The mines of Colorado are on a more substantial basis to-day than ever before. Reckless speculation and extravagant expenditure did much in the early days to shake confidence in the inherent richness of the mountains. Discoveries are continually making which rival their predecessors, and these, with the perfection and cheapening of processes for extraction of ores, and the erection of improved mills for the separation of base and valuable minerals, have increased mining operations. New districts are continually bidding for an influx of miners. Gilpin county, with her gold mines; Boulder county, with her gold deposits, and the Carbon silver district; Clear Creek county, with her great silver mines; Summit, Park and Lake counties, with their gold-bearing gulches and silver lodes; the San Juan mines, in southwestern Colorado; all these, and many other localities, are noted for their inexhaustible auriferous and argentiferous deposits. The annual product of gold and silver bullion in this territory is steadily increasing; a new era has set in which presages prosperity for this original and great industry of the Rocky Mountain region.

Within the past five years the colony system of settlement has developed itself, and met with great favor. In passing over the territory, we met with a number of these enterprises, some of which have grown into sterling communities under the direction of energetic men. The German Colonization Society, which was organized in Chicago in

1869, and settled in the Wet Mountain Valley, Fremont county, never succeeded in building itself up. The Union Colony, which was formed in New York in 1869, located at a point fifty-two miles from Denver, at the confluence of the Cache-a-la-Poudre and Platte rivers, and founded the city of Greeley, which is now one of the most prosperous localities in Colorado. The Chicago-Colorado Colony, in 1870, settled one mile from Burlington and fourteen miles from Boulder, and named their town Longmont. It is a thriving community. The St. Louis Western Colony was formed in 1870, and were joined by the New England Colony, of Boston, after which they fixed upon Evans, forty-eight miles below Denver, and four miles above Greeley, on the Platte, as their site. They have a pleasant city growing up, and are a praiseworthy community. A colony was organized at Memphis, Tennessee, in 1870, and named the Southwestern. It is located twenty-five miles below Greeley, on the Platte River. The Independence Colony was organized in 1871, and settled at New Memphis, on the Denver & Rio Grande Railway. In the same year a colony from Georgia settled on the Huerfano River, in southern Colorado. In 1871 the Fontaine Colony laid out the city of Colorado Springs, on the Denver & Rio Grande Railway, and have built up a thriving and important town. In 1873, the Fort Collins Colony was founded at Fort Collins, on the Cache-a-la-Poudre, twenty-five miles west of Greeley. It is thirty-two miles from Longmont, and twenty-two miles from Evans.

It is located in a rich agricultural region, and is destined to become a populous settlement. Another colony is located at Platteville, on the Platte River, between Evans and Denver. There is no reason why co-operation in land operations should not succeed in Colorado, and colonies, founded by reliable and trustworthy men, rapidly develop. Lands may be purchased reasonably, and thus, by a combination of effort, prosperous towns and thriving agricultural districts built up. This has been the flattering result of several of the colonization schemes spoken of.

In point of healthfulness, Colorado stands equal to the other favored sections of the globe. The territory has altitude, which gives her pure, electric, invigorating air, with low humidity, and is especially desirable, therefore, for invalids. With this are coupled beauty of scenery and brilliant sunshine, an even temperature and freedom from all miasmatic influences. Persons with bronchial affections, when they visit Colorado in the early stages of their complaints, invariably receive benefit. Other ailments are also greatly benefited. Physicians who have studied climatic conditions, and their effect upon various diseases, concede that in this territory is to be found the great sanitarium of the world. Colorado is yearly thronged with invalids, many of whom, finding themselves greatly helped, take up their permanent residence here. It is full of convalescents, who, almost as soon as they feel the mountain air, recuperate their energies and become strong once more.

Colorado is rich in mineral, in agricultural resources, mines, and progressive people. She is better known, and more justly appreciated than any other of the territorial domain. She is developing a high civilization, is fast becoming populated, and will, ere many years, take rank, for numerical strength, with many of the longer-settled States. Materially, the territory is incomparable.

THE END.

ADDENDA.

ADDENDA.

SUBJOINED is a table showing the approximate elevations above the sea level of the principal cities of Colorado, together with the leading summer resorts, mountain passes and noted peaks. The observations upon which the figures are based were made by Professors Hayden, Whitney, Guyot and Parry:

Points.	Feet.	Points.	Feet.
Boulder	5,536	Golden	5,642
Boulder Pass	11,700	Gray's Peak	14,254
Berthoud Pass	11,371	Georgetown	8,452
Central	8,300	Green Lake	11,000
Cañon City	4,700	Hot Springs	7,660
Caribou	9,167	Idaho Springs	7,800
Cheyenne Mountain	9,896	James' Peak	13,262
Chief, at Idaho Springs	11,716	Long's Peak	14,150
Colorado City	6,342	La Plata Mountain	14,188
Colorado Springs	5,872	Manitou	6,124
Denver	5,132	Massive Mountain	14,213
Estes' Park	7,528	Middle Park	8,690
Fairplay	9,854	Middle Boulder	8,067
Fall River	7,930	Mt. Byers	12,776
Grand Lake (Middle Park)	8,000	Mt. Evans	14,270

Points.	Feet.	Points.	Feet.
Mt. Elbert	14,222	Pike's Peak	13,985
Mt. Harvard	14,270	Pueblo	4,600
Mt. of Holy Cross	13,540	South Park	9,842
Mt. Lincoln	14,183	Sopris Peak	12,308
Mt. Powell	13,282	Torry's Peak	14,249
Mt. Rosalie	14,260	Twin Lakes	9,219
Mt. Silver Heels	13,794	Ute Pass	11,200
Mt. Yale	14,041	Uncompahgre Mountain	14,540

Below are the approximate populations of the leading cities in the Territory of Colorado, as based upon the most recent census, and the natural increase during the past year:

Cities.	Population.	Cities.	Population.
Black Hawk	2,500	Fort Collins	300
Boulder	1,000	Georgetown	2,200
Cañon City	700	Golden	1,400
Caribou	500	Granada	300
Central City	4,500	Greeley	2,000
Colorado City	300	Idaho Springs	300
Colorado Springs	1,000	Longmont	600
Del Norte	500	Manitou	300
Denver	20,000	Pueblo	3,000
Evans	800	Trinidad	1,200
Fairplay	500	West Las Animas	400

A statement of distances in miles between various points visited by travelers in Colorado may prove of great advantage, and also give a comprehensive idea of the extent of territory traversed in making excursions through the mountains:

ADDENDA.

From Denver to Golden, 17; to Black Hawk, 38; to Central, 39; to Nevada, 40; to Idaho, *via* Central, 46; *via* Floyd Hill, 40; to Fall River, 42½; to Georgetown, 55; to Middle Park, *via* Berthoud's Pass, 96; to Boulder, 28 by wagon, and 45 by rail; to Longmont, 58 miles; to Caribou, by wagon to Boulder, 48, and by rail and wagon, 66; to Central, *via* Caribou, 76; to Colorado Springs, 76; to Colorado City, 78½; to Manitou, 81 miles; to Pueblo, 120; to Cañon, 160; to Fairplay, *via* Turkey Creek Cañon, 95; to Greeley, 52; to Monument Park, 67; to Kansas City, 637; to Omaha, 622; to Chicago, 1,100; to St. Louis, 912; to New York, 1,980; to Cincinnati, 1,363; to Philadelphia, 1,922; to Boston, 2,401; to Fort Garland, 218; to Saguache, 222; to Los Piños Agency, 282; to Trinidad, 220.

From Idaho Springs to Fall River, 2½; to Georgetown, 13; to Berthoud's Pass, 16; to Hot Sulphur Springs, in Middle Park, 60; to Chicago Lakes, trail, 15; to Central City, *via* Virginia Cañon, 6; to Golden, 23; to Denver, 40; to Floyd Hill, railroad terminus, 5.

From Boulder to Denver, by rail, 45; to Golden, 28; to Longmont, 13; to Caribou, by wagon, 21; to Caribou Mill, 18; to Central, *via* Caribou, 30; to Georgetown, 49.

From Fairplay to Cañon City, 75; to Colorado Springs, *via* Ute Pass, 75; to Colorado Springs, *via* Cañon, 120; to Twin Lakes, *via* Salt Works, 75; to Twin Lakes, *via* Mountain Pass, 35.

From Georgetown to Green Lake, 2½; to summit of Gray's Peak, 15; to Hot Springs, in Middle Park, 45.

From Colorado Springs to Denver, 76; to Pueblo, 44; to Cañon City, 76; to Colorado City, 2½; to Manitou, 5; to Garden of the Gods, 4; to Glen Eyrie, 5; to Cheyenne Cañon, 5; to Monument, 8; to the Petrified Stumps, 30; to Fairplay, 77; to the summit of Pike's Peak, 16.

From Cañon City to local points — The Gate of the Arkansas Cañon, one-half mile; to the Main Cañon, 8; to the Mineral Springs, one-quarter mile; to the Warm Springs, one-half mile; to the Iron Rock Springs, 3½; to the Oil Wells, 6. To Fairplay, 75; to Denver, 160; to Pueblo, 40; to Colorado Springs, 84.

From Longmont to Long's Peak, 30; Greeley to Caribou, 59; Pueblo to Trinidad, 100; Pueblo to Santa Fe, New Mexico, 295; Fairplay to California Gulch, 35; Pueblo to the San Juan Mines, 200.

From Denver to Golden, 17; to Black Hawk, 38; to Central, 39; to Nevada, 40; to Idaho, *via* Central, 46; *via* Floyd Hill, 40; to Fall River, 42½; to Georgetown, 55; to Middle Park, *via* Berthoud's Pass, 96; to Boulder, 28 by wagon, and 45 by rail; to Longmont, 58 miles; to Caribou, by wagon to Boulder, 48, and by rail and wagon, 66; to Central, *via* Caribou, 76; to Colorado Springs, 76; to Colorado City, 78½; to Manitou, 81 miles; to Pueblo, 120; to Cañon, 160; to Fairplay, *via* Turkey Creek Cañon, 95; to Greeley, 52; to Monument Park, 67; to Kansas City, 637; to Omaha, 622; to Chicago, 1,100; to St. Louis, 912; to New York, 1,980; to Cincinnati, 1,363; to Philadelphia, 1,922; to Boston, 2,401; to Fort Garland, 218; to Saguache, 222; to Los Piños Agency, 282; to Trinidad, 220.

From Idaho Springs to Fall River, 2½; to Georgetown, 13; to Berthoud's Pass, 16; to Hot Sulphur Springs, in Middle Park, 60; to Chicago Lakes, trail, 15; to Central City, *via* Virginia Cañon, 6; to Golden, 23; to Denver, 40; to Floyd Hill, railroad terminus, 5.

From Boulder to Denver, by rail, 45; to Golden, 28; to Longmont, 13; to Caribou, by wagon, 21; to Caribou Mill, 18; to Central, *via* Caribou, 30; to Georgetown, 49.

From Fairplay to Cañon City, 75; to Colorado Springs, *via* Ute Pass, 75; to Colorado Springs, *via* Cañon, 120; to Twin Lakes, *via* Salt Works, 75; to Twin Lakes, *via* Mountain Pass, 35.

From Georgetown to Green Lake, 2½; to summit of Gray's Peak, 15; to Hot Springs, in Middle Park, 45.

From Colorado Springs to Denver, 76; to Pueblo, 44; to Cañon City, 76; to Colorado City, 2½; to Manitou, 5; to Garden of the Gods, 4; to Glen Eyrie, 5; to Cheyenne Cañon, 5; to Monument, 8; to the Petrified Stumps, 30; to Fairplay, 77; to the summit of Pike's Peak, 16.

From Cañon City to local points — The Gate of the Arkansas Cañon, one-half mile; to the Main Cañon, 8; to the Mineral Springs, one-quarter mile; to the Warm Springs, one-half mile; to the Iron Rock Springs, 3½; to the Oil Wells, 6. To Fairplay, 75; to Denver, 160; to Pueblo, 40; to Colorado Springs, 84.

From Longmont to Long's Peak, 30; Greeley to Caribou, 59; Pueblo to Trinidad, 100; Pueblo to Santa Fe, New Mexico, 295; Fairplay to California Gulch, 35; Pueblo to the San Juan Mines, 200.

ROCKY MOUNTAIN GEMS
AND
Colorado Gold Jewelry.

To the Tourist and Traveling Public.

—

Attention is called to the Large Assortment of

JEWELRY

Manufactured from

COLORADO GOLD

and

ROCKY MOUNTAIN GEMS

by

MOSS AGATE,
CRYSTAL,
TOPAZ,
GARNET,
AMETHYST,
OPAL,
PETRIFIED WOOD,

Constantly on hand, Set in

RINGS,
PINS,
SETS,
STUDS,
SLEEVE BUTTONS,
Chains, Charms, Etc.

A. B. INGOLS, JEWELER,
263 & 265 FIFTEENTH STREET,
DENVER.

Inter-Ocean Hotel

CORNER BLAKE AND SIXTEENTH STREETS,

DENVER, COLORADO.

The INTER-OCEAN HOTEL is the most centrally located in the city, modern in all its appointments, furnished with rooms en suite, Holmes' Telegraph Annunciator, hot and cold baths, private dining parlors, and in full view of the Rocky Mountains and all the prominent peaks.

This hotel is especially adapted for the comfort of invalids and families. Has ample accommodations for 250 guests.

Large and commodious sample rooms for the use of commercial men.

Best of livery in attendance at short notice and at reasonable rates.

Check agents of the Denver Transfer Company will pass through the trains and Check baggage for the INTER-OCEAN HOTEL, thus saving passengers the confusion at the depot.

Especial care will be given to the comfort of the guests, and entire satisfaction guaranteed in every particular by the proprietors.

H. C. CHAPIN.
M. B. GOODELL.

JAMES H. WALL, JR., formerly proprietor of Hoffman House, N. Y., Manager.

Fred L. Hahn.   Jno. C. Tucker.

Hahn, Tucker & Co.

DENVER

Real Estate & Mining Exchange,

Loan, Collection and Insurance Office,

243 Sixteenth Street,

DENVER, COLORADO.

Real Estate of all descriptions bought and sold. Loans of money negotiated on ample security, at the highest rates of interest, for residents and non-residents, in a careful and judicious manner. Especial care observed in the examination of Titles to Real Estate.

The largest and choicest list of City and Suburban Property for sale and for rent that can be found in Denver.

General Agents for Colorado for Diebold & Kienzle's Fire and Burglar Proof Safes and Vaults.

General Agents for The Mutual Life Insurance Company of New York, and The Brewers' Fire Insurance Company of Milwaukee, Wisconsin.

REFERENCES:

Collins, Snider & Co., Bankers, Denver.	Nelson Sargent,	Denver.
First National Bank, "	E. R. Wadsworth,	Chicago.
City National Bank, "	D. S. Covert,	"
Daniel Witter, "	Emil Baur,	Cincinnati.
F. J. Ebert, "	H. B. Merrell,	Detroit.
Wm. N. Clayton, "	F. S. Winston,	New York.
Wm. N. Byers, "	R. A. McCurdy,	"
Henry C. Brown, "	F. W. Vanuxen,	Philadelphia.

Colorado National Bank

OF DENVER, COLORADO.

UNITED STATES DEPOSITORY, AND SPECIALLY DESIGNATED AS A DEPOSITORY FOR THE FUNDS OF UNITED STATES DISBURSING OFFICERS.

Authorized Capital, - - - $500,000
Capital paid in, - - - - 100,000

DIRECTORS:

Augustus Kountze, - - President.
Charles B. Kountze, - Vice-President.
Wm. B. Berger, - - - - Cashier.
S. N. Wood, - - Assistant Cashier.
A. B. Daniels.

Does a general Banking and Exchange Business, buying and selling domestic and foreign exchange, gold dust, gold and silver, and United States securities of all kinds. County and local securities of all kinds bought and sold.

Receives deposits, allowing interest on time deposits. Commercial and business paper discounted, and all the usual facilities of the Banking Business extended to customers.